FOUR GOSPELS, FOUR HEARTS, ONE LORD

Four Gospels, Four Hearts, One Lord

READING MATTHEW, MARK, LUKE, & JOHN IN CONTEXT

BY ADDISON HODGES HART

Angelico Press

First published in the USA
by Angelico Press 2025
Copyright © By Addison Hodges Hart 2025

For information, address:
Angelico Press, Ltd.
169 Monitor St.
Brooklyn, NY 11222
www.angelicopress.com

ppr 979-8-89280-152-2
cloth 979-8-89280-153-9

Book and cover design
by Michael Schrauzer

Dedicated with affection to the
All Saints Sisters of the Poor
in Catonsville, Maryland

Contents

I

The Gospels In Their
Original Context

T he apostles ("emissaries") of Jesus were the central figures of that network of "assemblies" that would first receive the name "Christian" in the city of Antioch. The most notable among that company were James, "the brother of the Lord," Kephas (Simon Peter), and John, the son of Zebedee. It was Paul—a latecomer among those called "apostles"—who referred to these three as the "pillars" of the church (Gal. 2:9). However, by the end of the first century, two were esteemed above the rest: Peter and alongside him—rather surprisingly—Paul. So vital were these two to the subsequent growth of the church that we may justifiably call the Christian Tradition as we know it in all its varieties essentially "Petrine-Pauline." Every ecclesial offshoot springing from the original apostolic stem in those earliest centuries was either to disappear as a viable community or to reintegrate eventually into the main "Petrine-Pauline" Tradition.

The ensuing centrality of Paul is, as I said, somewhat surprising, considering his former reputation. His claim to apostleship rankled some: he had, after all, initially been a ferocious opponent of the new sect. But he had had an encounter with the risen Christ (described three times in the book of Acts: 9:1–19a; 22:6–11; 26:9–23;[1] see

---

[1] I agree entirely with Pauline scholar Douglas A. Campbell that the book of Acts was written by an eyewitness. As Campbell has written, "Acts is highly accurate for an ancient historian's work. In fact, I think that this is only explicable with the realization that for much of the time the author was there, as from time to time the

Paul's own claim that this was a revelation of Jesus's resurrection in 1 Corinthians 9:1; 15:5–11), which convinced
him that he had been in the wrong and must instead
now proclaim to others the Lord he had formerly reviled.
Before the close of that same century, some decades
after his execution in AD 64, Paul's letters were being
collected and read as scripture by the *ekklesia* he had once
persecuted (we see this attested to in the New Testament
itself: 2 Peter 3:16). Second only to Jesus, Paul is the most
pivotal figure in church history, his writings constituting
about a quarter of the New Testament canon.[2] Although
this is a book about the four canonical Gospels, and not
about Paul's letters, it must be said nevertheless that we
cannot understand those Gospels without Paul or the
Petrine-Pauline Tradition.

I must dismiss a common misconception before continuing. It was G. L. Prestige, a scholar of great value
but barely remembered these days, who identified this

---

narrative suggests" (see Acts 16:10–17; and 20:6 to the conclusion
of the book in chapter 28). *Paul: An Apostle's Journey* (Grand Rapids,
2018). All of Campbell's Pauline scholarship is worth reading.

[2] I am fully conscious of the fact that the authenticity of some
of the epistles of Paul is disputed (2 Thessalonians, Ephesians,
Colossians) and some rejected as such by many modern NT scholars (1 and 2 Timothy, Titus). In recent years, I have returned
to the presupposition that *all* the canonical letters attributed to
Paul are authentic, and the perceived differences in their styles
and theology can be accounted for by less drastic explanations
than assuming "forgery" (but even when later writers did write
in the guise of well-known earlier figures, the ancient practice
was clearly not regarded as "forgery" in any culpable sense). The
Pastoral Epistles in particular are viewed as inauthentic. Nonetheless, the arguments for their possible authenticity advanced
by the renowned scholar of early Christianity J. N. D. Kelly have
never been satisfactorily explained away in my estimation—and
until they are, I stubbornly adhere to my position. See J. N. D.
Kelly, *The Pastoral Epistles*, Black's New Testament Commentaries
(London, 1963) 3–34. It is notable that, since Kelly's time, the New
Testament scholar Luke Timothy Johnson has also defended the
Pauline authorship of the Pastoral Epistles.

mistake in historical biblical criticism as long ago as 1940; yet it is still with us and informs the thinking of far too many who have undertaken New Testament and early Christian studies. Prestige discussed what "tradition" (*traditio, paradosis*) is and, in so doing, listed some of the prejudices leveled against those who stood accused of being theological "traditionalists" (a pejorative) within the academy. I won't reproduce Prestige's argument here, except to note the last point he makes in it, which deals specifically with New Testament scholarship and the sort of "eisegesis" (meaning the lamentable tendency to *read into* a text or historical data rather than to *read out of* it; the latter discipline is properly called "exegesis") that still haunts NT scholarship in our own day—lingering like the "faint odours of departed cheese," to quote Lewis Carroll, who knew a thing or two about academic affectations. Here is Prestige, and note the irony he sharply employs:

> There may even be a moral stigma attached to [the "traditionalist" theologian/scholar] for "preferring the traditions of the elders" to the pure and original truth [so-called, I may add]. The implication is that those Christians who value tradition inevitably corrupt their recognized principles in the course of public transmission; and that dogmatic antiques are therefore *only reputable if they are already lost to sight before St. Paul wrote his epistles and have been completely buried in oblivious sands for the intervening nineteen centuries. Truth, on this view, includes only what nineteen centuries have forgotten or what the twentieth century has itself invented.*[3]

What Prestige meant was simply this: there are scholars who prefer to "invent" what they surmise "must" have been the historical realities shaping "the Jesus movement" before Paul came along and "invented" Christianity.

---

[3] G. L. Prestige, D. D., *Fathers and Heretics: Six Studies in Dogmatic Faith with Prologue and Epilogue, being The Bampton Lectures for 1940* (London, 1940), 2. Emphasis mine.

Today that tendency among New Testament critics and historians of early Christianity is very much worse than it was in Prestige's day. I will make two quick points, then, before coming directly to the subject of this book:

First, there is no gap between "the historical Jesus" and Paul or the book of Acts. There's no "*there* there" that can be explored. Second, the *only* doorway that is, in fact, open to us for gaining genuine understanding of the Christian faith in its earliest form is the "Petrine-Pauline" or "apostolic" Tradition that we have already briefly noted. It *is* the tradition from which *everything else* derives, be it liturgy, piety, mystical theology, the creeds, or even the New Testament writings themselves.

With those two assertions flatly stated and gotten out of the way, let us reflect on the following scenario.

Imagine, if you will, that you are a member of one of the first-century communities of those who affirm Jesus of Nazareth as the "Anointed One" ("Messiah," "Christ"), the Son of God. Not only that, you stand within that pristine tradition — only a matter of decades after your small assembly (*ekklesia*) was established — that honors Peter and Paul as your two foundational apostles. Perhaps there are other communities of followers of Christ in the same region in which you dwell, who look to other apostolic founders. But your congregation has a special relationship with the Christians in Rome, where both Peter and Paul were martyred. The old mother community in Jerusalem has been scattered in the wake of catastrophic events there, so Rome's churches have taken center stage.

You have been baptized and initiated into the mysteries of union with Christ. You have, in other words, along with all your fellow Christians, "died" and been "raised" in baptism, and now you are living "in Christ" and he is living in you. You are part of his "body." Consequently, you are no longer part of this *kosmos* ("world") or this *aion* ("age"), and your true life is "hidden with Christ in

God." You mystically breathe with his "Spirit" ("Breath") and have entered into a continuous process of personal transformation that will reach its fulfilment in "the age to come." You practice a disciplined routine of prayer (possibly one that includes expressions of the ecstatic), share a sacred meal with your companions, are involved in acts of charity for the poor, the widowed, the sick, orphans, and others. Above all, you live in the conviction that Jesus is alive, truly present in the midst of your gatherings, the physician and shepherd of your soul, and will be your merciful judge when the end of this present age comes. Thus, when your community shares again either the oral or written record of Jesus's acts and words, you are heart and soul present to it. You are, in a sense, *there*; Jesus is speaking to his *ekklesia* directly once again, and so he is speaking directly to *you*. The Spirit enlivens the story, and it isn't only *Jesus*'s story, but as a member of his body, it's also *your* story.

Such a conviction of real union between the living Christ and his followers is captured in passages of the New Testament. Romans 6:3–11, for example:

> Do you not know that all of us who have been baptized into Christ Jesus were baptized into his death? We were buried therefore with him by baptism into death, so that as Christ was raised from the dead by the glory of the Father, we too might walk in newness of life. For if we have been united [literally, *planted/grown together*] with him in a death like his [through the immersion of baptism], we shall certainly be united with him in a resurrection like his. We know that our old self was crucified with him so that the sinful body might be destroyed, and we might no longer be enslaved to sin. For he who has died is freed from sin. But if we have died with Christ, we believe that we shall also live with him. For we know that Christ being raised from the dead will never die again; death no longer has dominion over him. The death he died he died to sin, once for all, but the life he lives he lives to God.

So you also must consider yourselves dead to sin and
alive to God in Christ Jesus.[4]

Here we have a particularly strong affirmation of the
disciple's *total identification* with Jesus Christ. Paul could
say of himself, reversing the image of being "in Christ"
to Christ being "in him" and meaning by that reversal
much the same thing, "[I]t is no longer I who live, but
Christ who lives in me" (Gal. 2:20). As we will see, when
we look at the Gospel of Mark, this identification of the
life of the disciple and Jesus is a significant, often overlooked, interpretive key to that book.

In another of his epistles, Paul even boldly asserts in
clearly metaphorical language that the baptized follower
no longer inwardly or essentially exists on this plane at all:

If then you have been raised with Christ, seek the
things that are above, where Christ is, seated at the
right hand of God. Set your minds on things that
are above, not on things that are on earth. For you
have died, and your life is hid with Christ in God.
When Christ who is our life appears, then you also
will appear with him in glory. (Colossians 3:1–4)

I provide a picture of this vital context, out of which
the four canonical Gospels (which are the earliest Gospels
we have, although there were others) emerged, because I
propose in this short book to explore what can be called
their *mystical* dimension. By "mystical" I mean—again to
use Paul's words—a deep engagement with "the *mystery*
[formerly] hidden for ages and generations but *now made
manifest* to [Christ's] saints" (Col. 1:26; emphasis added;
the word *saints* refers to those "made holy"—*those set
apart from the world*—by the Spirit, through baptism and
faith). Christian mysticism was never intended to be the
preserve of a spiritual elite; rather it is a *gnosis*—i.e., a
participative knowledge—made manifest through the Holy

---

[4] All English translations are taken from the Revised Standard
Version, unless otherwise indicated.

Spirit to all who seek to follow the Way of Jesus. It isn't arcane or esoteric knowledge; it is *revelation* — meaning *something disclosed*. In other words, it is not obscure or hidden away, made available only to a select few among the faithful. Its primary and continuous feature is repentance — *metanoia* — which literally means the reorienting and transformation of one's mind/thoughts/heart, and it is proclaimed *to all*. Everything the disciple does in thought, word, and deed is to become, in an unspoiled sense, authentically *mystical*, a manifesting of Christ before the world.

It is important that we understand right at the outset, then, that *the Gospels were read within gatherings whose members understood themselves precisely in the terms described above.*

The Gospels were not evangelistic tracts for unbelievers, but rather histories for the committed, in which the latter understood themselves to be mystically *participative*. It cannot be stressed enough that these books were not primarily addressed to those outside the *ekklesia*. They were written down for those who were either already baptized or on the way to baptism, and for the earliest generations of followers of the Way, they were not yet even written down. The Tradition was originally oral, and — even though it was not an esoteric teaching in the "secret society" sense — it was nonetheless protected from the full scrutiny of the uninitiated (a fact that was to lead, of course, to misunderstanding and calumny by suspicious outsiders). As I write in the first appendix in this book, "The four Gospels became canonical (the word 'canon' means something by which we measure other things) for good reason: they were the ones the vast majority of Christians treasured most and regarded as genuinely representing Jesus as they experienced him. They constituted the original apostolic deposit, *the authentic tradition* as written."

The guardedness against the prying eyes of outsiders that I mentioned reflected Christ's words to his

apostles: "To you has been given *the secret* of the kingdom
of God, but for those outside everything is in parables"
(Mark 4:11; emphasis added). Parables are sayings and
stories that demand serious attention from the hearers if
they are to be interpreted rightly. We can assume that for
those who heard the basic revelatory proclamation (what
was called the *kerygma*) about God's coming judgment
and Jesus's resurrection, but rejected it, the door to the
church was firmly barred.

The earliest of the written Gospels that are extant is
assumed by most scholars to be the one attributed to
Mark. We do not know, of course, whether or not that
assumption is accurate; there are reputable arguments
to the contrary. But for simplicity's sake, I follow the
majority view here. In the very first verse of Mark's Gospel
(which may not, in fact, have been its original first verse),
we find the word "gospel," meaning a proclamation of
"glad tidings" or "good news," employed to describe what
the book contains. It's noteworthy that the Greek word
translated as "gospel" — εὐαγγέλιον ("*euaggelion*") — was
Paul's favorite word to designate the message he preached.
Perhaps the use of the word was a reference to Isaiah 52:7,
in which God's reign is proclaimed as good news. It was
a word used in the Roman world, as well, to announce
benefits bestowed by the emperor, although that particular usage might post-date Paul's use of the term. An
earlier use of the word dates to the time of Augustus
(who was considered a god, a savior, and a ruler even of
the natural order), in celebration of the latter's birth. The
word *euaggelion* in a Messianic communal context, then,
might have been understood as countering the imperial claims (just as the designation, "empire" — βασιλεία
("*basileia*"), "of God" — which we usually see translated
as "kingdom of God" in English, implicitly was a counter
to the "kingdom" or "empire" of Rome). Paul meant by
the word *euaggelion* an actual verbal proclamation, but the
later designation when applied to the written accounts

of Jesus's life suggests that those hearing them regarded themselves as — inwardly, at least — the subjects of a quite different sort of "empire" than Rome's. Justin Martyr (c. 100–c. 165) referred to them most frequently as the apostles' "memoirs," although he sometimes called them "Gospels" as well.[5]

If one had asked a member of these earliest Christian assemblies whether he or she considered the "memoirs" they heard read aloud in their midst to be history or biography, the answer would have been "Yes." If they had been asked whether they regarded these accounts to be rich in mystical or spiritual meaning, the answer would have been the same. We must bear in mind that ancient people didn't view historiography as we do today. They saw it, and history itself, as *significant* — that is to say, they saw history as the bearer of *signs* and *symbols*. Mere facts were not as vitally important to them as was the underlying *truth* that provided the foundation for communal, and therefore personal, *meaning*. That the Gospels are not the kind of historiography to which we're accustomed is indicated by how much of Jesus's biography they do *not* provide — and this lack of interest in what we would consider essential aspects of biographical background today was the norm in ancient historical writing. As I noted above, the Gospel they heard *included* the hearers; it was *their* story because they were one with and in Christ. As we've noted already, the followers of Jesus understood their baptismal union — *at-one-ment* — with Jesus as inclusion in his corporate "body." This is made shockingly obvious, for example, when Paul warns the Christians at Corinth against sexual immorality in these striking terms: "Do you not know that *your bodies* are members of Christ? Shall I therefore take *the members of Christ* and make them members of a prostitute? Never!"

---

[5] See Justin's *First Apology*, 66.3; 67.3; *Dialogue with Trypho the Jew*, 10.2; 100.1; 100.4; 101.3; 102.5; 103.6, 8; 104.1; 105.1, 5, 6; 106.1, 3, 4; 107.1.

(1 Cor. 6:15; emphasis added). Such was the concrete nature of their union with Christ. Atonement was not merely a matter of doctrinal belief; it involved the whole psychosomatic self.

Regarding the matter of history, a caveat is in order. At the very least, it will indicate what I fully intend to avoid in this book, which is *historicism*. Anyone truly seeking to understand the Gospels or the Christian Tradition in all their depth, complexity, and insight should be wary of historicism, a prejudice that underlies much historical writing but rarely is acknowledged as the philosophical guiding principle it is. Too often it slips under the radar unnoticed by even the most discerning readers — and it really shouldn't be ignored or get a pass. *Historicism is not the same thing as the study of history*. Rather, it presupposes a philosophical-materialist prejudice that *all* phenomena, beliefs, and convictions must be explained solely in terms of historical development (as Benedetto Croce put it, historicism is "the affirmation that life and reality are *history alone*" — my emphasis). This idea developed in Europe during the nineteenth century, with Germany leading the way. Historicism is the sibling of scientism, the belief that all phenomena can be explained by science, again as understood in terms of philosophical materialism. Taken for granted in both historicism and scientism is *the implicit denial of any transcendent reality* — a denial based entirely on prejudice. To make an ideologically materialist view of history or science the sole arbiter of such metaphysical categories as "God" or "Truth" is a "category mistake." History and science are of immeasurable value for humanity, of course, but only when they don't intrude upon those areas of human existence that are well beyond their purview.

Considering all this, what do we make of Jesus, who has been a favorite subject of historicists since the dawn of historicism? The first thing that should be acknowledged is that *historicism cannot contain him*. Any purely historicist

view of Jesus — the so-called "Jesus of history" as distinct
from the so-called "Christ of faith" — is inevitably going
to founder on a few stubbornly immoveable obstacles.
Chief among these unyielding facts is that no matter
how often or how many scholars and speculative fanta-
sists have tried — repeatedly and for centuries now — to
force a round Jesus into some conveniently square category, either "ancient" or contemporary or (not infre-
quently) invented, he never actually fits. He defies easy
categorization and always has. He has been depicted as
an apocalyptic prophet, a wisdom teacher, a magician, a
revolutionary, "woke," a mushroom cult leader, a pacifist,
a gnostic sage, a cultural conservative, an upholder of
nationalistic interests, and so on. But what seems to be
the most salient feature of the earliest records we have
about Jesus (the New Testament, in other words) is that
he defied expectations repeatedly during his life and afterwards. The uncomfortable fact for many scholars is that,
quite probably, *he really and truly was unclassifiable from the
very beginning* ("All things have been delivered to me by
my Father; and no one knows the Son except the Father,
and no one knows the Father except the Son and any one
to whom the Son chooses to reveal him"; Matt. 11:27). If
this really was the case with Jesus — and the only extant
evidence we possess strongly suggests that it was — then
historicist scholars with their concocted reconstructions
of the past and their catalog of neat categories to fit Jesus
into are hopelessly at a disadvantage (though possibly
at an advantage where the industry of "historical Jesus"
book-publishing is concerned).

Consider the single event that has been regarded as
the most important datum about Jesus — that he rose
from the dead and was encountered after his death, even
by multiple persons at once. Even if we second-guess
the conviction that he repeatedly appeared to people
after his ignominious execution, appealing to various
mythologies or to Jewish belief in the resurrection as

influencing it, we are still left with those hard claims that he was alive and, in some way, *present*, and with the undeniable fact that his movement continued and flourished in this firm belief. The entire body of early Christian literature testifies to it. At this point, the genuinely honest historian or scientist really has very little to say; neither is competent to address the truth or not of a matter that transcends the strictly material. And though the early Christians' belief in Jesus's imminent return after his ascension proved premature, the conviction of his *abiding presence* persisted. By the time the final editing of the Gospel of John is supposed to have been completed (most scholars assume it was sometime near the close of the first century), for a sizeable portion of Christians the belief in a pending *parousia* had evolved into the deeper conviction that, in Jesus's incarnation ("en-flesh-ment"), death, and resurrection, the *eschaton* (the End) *had already been realized*: eternal life had *already* entered into the cosmos with its penetrating and transformative power. The future resurrection was *already* at work in human lives. The "second coming" was not the immediate concern; the *presence* of Jesus through the Holy Spirit was the most essential — and essentially *lived*, *worshipped*, and *prayed* — experience of the baptized. *This* is what became the mainstream belief of the church — and, unfortunately for the modern historicist, it is no longer a theoretical question concerning history, but an empirical and practical mystical knowledge that evades understanding by sheerly rationalistic means.

In other words, the original Tradition must be treated as a mystery to be entered into and only there *realized*. Its meaning cannot be appreciated by those who attempt to evaluate it "objectively" from the outside. The message is "Come and see" (John 1:46) — "come and experience." Without this, the Tradition is unknowable, and all that is accessible to the outsider is external data, the empirical significance of which (try as he might) he will never truly "get." Original Christian experience, from baptism onward, was — as we've seen — immersive and absorbing, not a coolly distant consideration of concepts. We can either unfold through experience what that Tradition reveals, or mangle its meaning with the historicist's much-too-tiny wringer. Speaking for myself, I can't be bothered with the latter.

Returning then to what exactly a Gospel was understood to be in the earliest Christian communities, then, Robert M. Grant had this to say:

> Ancient Christians had in mind a picture of [Jesus] with a "historical" life, but they were not primarily interested in dealing with that life either by using psychological techniques or by employing historical tools to analyse the setting in time and place. They did not ask themselves, as we might ask ourselves of any historical character, what it was his nature to be and to do. They did not try to make Jesus comprehensible against his environment in the manner of a modern biographer. And once they had decided not only that Jesus himself was the divine logos but also that the sources for his life were written under divine inspiration, all the presuppositions which might make a "biographical" interest possible had disappeared.[6]

Indeed, the Gospel attributed to John is explicit about what will ignite the disciples' later "remembering": it is the Holy Spirit who will awaken in their memories what Jesus said and did, and do so in such a way that their deeper significance is revealed ("But the Counselor, the Holy Spirit, whom the Father will send in my name, he will teach you all things, and bring to your remembrance all that I have said to you"; John 14:26). Origen (c. 185–c. 253), who can hardly be described as a "liberal" theologian in the modern sense, could write with absolutely no qualms that the writers of the Gospels

---

[6] Robert M. Grant, *The Earliest Lives of Jesus* (New York, 1961), 2.

made full use for their purpose of things done by Jesus in the exercise of his wonderful and extraordinary power; they use in the same way his sayings, and in some places they tack on to their writing, with language apparently implying things of sense, things made manifest to them in a purely intellectual way. I do not condemn them if they even sometimes dealt freely with things which to the eye of history happened differently, and changed them so as to serve the mystical aims they had in view...They proposed to speak the truth where it was possible both materially and spiritually, and where this was not possible it was their intention to prefer the spiritual to the material. The spiritual truth was often preserved, as one might say, in the material falsehood.[7]

Origen's bold statement is not asserting that the writers merely "made stuff up." Rather, he is stressing something that people of that age took in their stride: *spiritual truth was more important than material facts.* If spiritual truth is best conveyed by shaping a story to communicate it more clearly, so be it. The *mystical* sense is of utmost importance.

This same mentality is seen in Irenaeus of Lyons' (b. 131) defense of the four—and only four—canonical Gospels. Irenaeus is often anachronistically misrepresented as a sort of fearsome "hammer of heretics" in the style of the Inquisition a millennium later, absurdly caricatured as a persecutor of "Gnostics," going about, if not destroying, at least demeaning writings he deemed dangerous (including, of course, those apocryphal Gospels that never made the final cut). That distortion is an unjust latter-day fabrication, and we would do right to trash it. That said, Irenaeus did write that "it is not possible that the Gospels can be either more or fewer in number than they are"—an opinion that to our ears today might be

---

[7] Origen, *Commentary on the Gospel of John*, Bk. X, Ch. 4 (cf. *Ante-Nicene Fathers*, vol. 9 [Peabody, 1999], 383).

less than compelling. But his rationale was not to pull a ready-made but lame excuse out of his hat for excluding writings that didn't meet his approval. The persuasiveness of his argument would have been, in his day, quite real, resting as it did on its mystical quality. Numbers carried deep significance in the ancient world (we might note that Jesus embraces a similar numerological mysticism in Mark 8:17–21, when that text is read carefully). Irenaeus continues:

> For, since there are four zones of the world in which we live, and four principal winds, while the Church is scattered throughout all the world, and the "pillar and ground" of the Church is the Gospel and the spirit of life; it is fitting that one should have four pillars, breathing out immortality on every side, and vivifying men afresh...For the cherubim, too, were four-faced, and their faces were images of the dispensation of the Son of God...And therefore the Gospels are in accord with these things, among which Christ Jesus is seated.[8]

Such an argument, as already noted, may wrongly appear to us to be Irenaeus's method of imposing orthodoxy, but this passage comes from a book written in an age long before the church had any real power to enforce her dogmas. Irenaeus was seeking to defend the well-attested "school" he was tasked to protect at whatever cost to himself, the credentials of which were sound and incontestable, against other, less credible "schools" — and a rival "school" is what a "heresy" technically was in Irenaeus's day. Within his own context, Irenaeus's line of reasoning amounted to a solid enough claim. And, as we have said, the Gospels were read and interpreted *mystically* within a community of those who saw themselves as entirely — body, soul, and spirit — "in Christ."

---

[8] Irenaeus of Lyons, *Against Heresies*, bk. 3, chap. 11, sec. 8. See also *Ante-Nicene Fathers*, vol. 1 (Peabody, 1999), 428.

2.

In the pages that follow, as far as I'm able, I intend to approach the Gospels "mystically" and "in Christ." The perennial Christian view has been that, interpreted outside the broad Tradition in which all four originated, their significance cannot adequately be ascertained ("[T]hough we have known Christ after the flesh, yet now henceforth know we him no more"; 2 Cor. 5:16, KJV). They are not mere works of biography, much less works of philosophy, spirituality, or religion. Christians regard them as revelation, and as essentially integrated even when the variations between them are visible at a surface level. Through them, the living Christ—fully God and fully man—speaks to those "with ears to hear," that is, with ears opened by the Spirit ("But the Counselor, the Holy Spirit, whom the Father will send in my name, he will teach you all things, and bring to your remembrance all that I have said to you"; John 14:26).[9]

This slim book is certainly not an extensive commentary, but a series of short studies. Each Gospel will have a handful of passages and themes teased out and surveyed, and what I intend to do is highlight distinctive aspects in each that don't often get more than cursory treatment. Again, I will approach them with the Tradition in mind, trying to "see" in these writings what *significance* (by which I mean "signs" that are there to be construed) they may have conveyed to the faithful.

The first thing to understand about the Gospels is that they were written to present *who Jesus is* to the congregations, as the apostles had proclaimed him. Each Gospel places great emphasis on the events that led to Jesus's crucifixion and resurrection, but what was also important to the Gospel writers was imparting the knowledge of just *who* it was who had appeared, suffered ignominiously, and proved ultimately to be victorious. Although it is a

---

[9] For an overview of biblical interpretation, see Appendix I.

theory in interpretation, it seems likely that the use of the literary chiasmus—constituting the textual "shape" of each Gospel—was intended to indicate the revelation of Jesus's identity.

Ancient literature frequently made use of this textual structure. To explain it simply, it means that a text has an A-B-(C)-B-A arrangement. In other words, a text is shaped "architecturally" like a literary "X" (in Greek, "X" is the letter "*chi*," hence "chiasmus," or "chiasm"), where the A-B themes or words in the first half of a text are mirrored by the B-A themes or words in the latter half. An example in a simple sentence might be Mercutio's remark in *Romeo and Juliet* (Act I, Scene IV) that "if love be rough with you, be rough with love." Here, it's merely the words "love" and "rough" that are then paralleled in reverse order. In the ancient world, and still in many cultures today, the chiasmic shape can be seen almost everywhere. It orders not only smaller units within a text, but—more complicatedly—entire texts themselves.

In each of the Gospels, there is an overall chiastic structure that has an *unmatched* text at the center, *the heart* (the *C* in the A-B-(C)-B-A arrangement noted above). The importance of the textual "heart," when one appears in the text (or, in the case of Luke–Acts, a connecting "hinge" motif; more about that in due course), is indicated by its being the *only* section in the book without any discernible parallel. Hence, that *unparalleled center* becomes especially significant—a vital key to understanding rightly the significance of the complete work. In the Gospels, each of these centers indicates *who* and *what* Jesus is. Each is a revelation of the one who has come into the world and endures the cross.[10]

Although John's Gospel has the most elaborate chiastic structure of the four, we will see it in the Gospel of Mark—our first stop in this short tour—even though it's

---

[10] For an enlightening website that deals extensively with this subject, see: http://www.bible.literarystructure.info/bible/bible_e.html.

not a certainty that we have either the original beginning or end of that work. That said, what lies at its heart seems evident, and it also indicates that Mark's book isn't as grim and downbeat as some modern commentators have suggested (the Gospel ends abruptly, with a few women hastening from Jesus's empty tomb in consternation and saying nothing about their experience: a clear indication, I believe, that the original ending was lost). Indeed, the narrative overall is quite the opposite.

But we will come to that in our next chapter.

II

The Gospel of Mark

1.

T here is a timeworn theme that has gained some traction in recent times in popular discussions about early Christianity and the New Testament. It's the idea that Jesus and Paul (to the disadvantage of the latter) should be viewed as fundamentally at odds in their teachings. Certainly, there are conspicuous distinctions between Jesus and Paul, ignoring of course the most obvious, that of their respective statuses within the early *ekklesia* (there's a vast difference, after all, between the one proclaimed as the Messiah and the one who called himself the former's "apostle" and even likened his apostolic status to that of "a miscarried baby"; see 1 Cor. 15:8). These distinctions would include the following: Jesus had been a man of the countryside, dirt poor, a worker, a Galilean, and his first language had been Aramaic (although a knowledge of Greek seems likely). Paul, on the other hand, was a man from the important, Stoicism-soaked city of Tarsus in Cilicia (in Asia Minor), highly learned, whose first language was Greek, although he also knew Hebrew, Aramaic, and possibly a modicum of Latin. These are all marked dissimilarities between the two. From the writings we have, we can likewise see that Jesus's teachings, especially as we find them in the Synoptic Gospels, and Paul's have sometimes strikingly different (though not clashing) emphases and styles. In fact, the one epistle in the whole New Testament canon that comes closest to propounding the unadorned teachings we find in the Synoptics, especially those in Matthew, is the Letter of James.[1]

---

[1] See my 2018 book, *The Letter of James: A Pastoral Commentary* (Wipf & Stock).

Nevertheless, there is a seemingly tendentious trend to force a significant wedge between Jesus and Paul where, as a matter of simple historical fact, a wedge doesn't fit.

I say this for one obvious reason: when it comes to the Gospels, as we noted in the last chapter, *all* of them were accepted as authoritative in contexts where Paul had been an important influence—if not directly, then certainly indirectly. To put the matter differently, *if* a book appears in the NT *at all*, it is because it is viewed as being in accord with the tradition of Peter *and Paul* (this is even true of the Letter of James, which appears to be critical of the dangers of an exaggerated Paulinism).

More to the point, the early Christians who read in their gatherings the four canonical Gospels did so—again, as we saw in the previous chapter—*within the same conceptual universe that we find enunciated in Paul's writings.* We have already looked briefly at that conceptual universe, which at its core is mystical in nature. At the end of the day, after all the dust has settled surrounding what we know, or think we know, or feel that we want to be true about the historical Jesus, what we still have to work with foundationally are the Gospels in the New Testament— all four of which were written in Greek (not Aramaic, the language of Jesus), all written after the deaths of Peter and Paul in Rome, and all sharing in a broad, inclusive tradition indebted to those two apostles in particular (see Appendix I, especially the section dealing with the shape of the New Testament canon). Despite the internal differences between the Gospels themselves, they hold together precisely because they coinhere in the same broad tradition. And that tradition is, as I said, inherently *mystical.* As we look, then, at the first of our Gospels in this series—that attributed to Mark—these basic facts should be borne in mind, even when they go unsaid explicitly.

Although some have proposed Galilee or Syria as the location of that Gospel's composition, and although there is a strong (if perhaps legendary) association of Mark himself with Alexandria in Egypt (where, evidence suggests, there existed possibly three versions of the Marcan Gospel), the most likely place for its origin seems to be Rome. Of the four Gospels, it's unclear that either Matthew or John wrote the Gospels attributed to them; in the cases of Mark and Luke, however, there is a stronger possibility that the Gospels that go under their names are rightly attributed. In the case of Mark, tradition identifies him as the "John Mark" mentioned in the book of Acts, also mentioned in the Letter to the Colossians (12:12, 25; 13:5; 15:37–39; Col. 4:10), or the "Mark, my son" of 1 Peter 5:13. Mark's Gospel has always been linked to the preaching of Peter; the earliest attestation of this appears as early as circa 120 (see Eusebius, *Ecclesiastical History* 3.39.15). So, we have external evidence that the Gospel was written by "Mark" in Rome, and we also have internal evidence. As summarized by Raymond E. Brown:

> The gospel explains Aramaic expressions (3:17; 5:41; 7:11, etc.) and elementary Jewish customs (7:3–5), so that Palestine as place of composition may be plausibly excluded. There are more Latinisms [transliterations] in the Greek of Mark than in any other gospel, and that statistic suggests an environment where Latin was frequently spoken.[2] In particular, it has been argued that the bronze *kodantres* coin of Mark 12:42, "the two *lepta* which constitute one *quadrans*," was not in circulation in the eastern section of the empire, so that Mark could be offering a coinage equivalent for western readers. Mark 15:21 identifies Simon of Cyrene as "the father of Alexander and Rufus," presumably because these two sons are known to Mark and his readers; and attention has been called to the only other Rufus in the NT who lives at Rome (Rom. 16:13), but the identification is adventurous.[3]

---

[2] *Prætorium, legio, denarius, census, centurio, speculator, quadrans,* and *sextarius* (in the form *xestes*). In 15:15, he translates into Greek the Latin phrase *satis facere* ("to satisfy").

[3] Raymond E. Brown and John P. Meier, *Antioch and Rome: New Testament Cradles of Catholic Christianity* (New York: Ramsey, 1983), 196–97.

In addition to these clues, the teaching on divorce in 10:10–12 reflects Roman law, under which a wife in certain circumstances could divorce her husband. In short, the internal evidence supports the external evidence, and the best guess is that the Gospel was written in Rome and by someone named "Mark" (a common name, as it happens). Its emphasis on "taking up one's cross" to become a disciple, the apocalyptic focus in Chapter 13 on "the end," and the lengthy final section about Jesus's condemnation, death, and the empty tomb have suggested to scholars that the community was faced with persecution or the threat of persecution, which *might* reflect a specifically Roman context. But as we noted in the previous post, the mystical identification of the disciple with Jesus through the "death, burial, and resurrection" of baptism could also explain this emphasis—and, as we will see, there is the possibility that one obscure feature in the text might point to that very interpretation (but we will get to that later in the chapter).

Mark's Gospel is fast-paced (he uses the Greek word for "immediately"—εὐθύς, "*euthys*"—forty-one times) and it's the shortest of the four (perhaps the reason why Mark was, according to tradition, called "the stump-fingered"). The Greek is rough, the sort one might have heard on the streets of Rome, and the grammar switches from present to past tense throughout.

Jesus's personal rough edges are also on display: in effect, he inelegantly tells demons and even the unruly forces of nature to "shut up" (literally, "be muzzled": 1:25; 4:39), bodily throws raucous intruders out the door in one notable scene (5:40), and he frequently shows anger and—in Gethsemane—a state of depression ("...he began to be greatly distressed and troubled, and he said to them, 'My soul is very sorrowful, even to death...'"; 14:33b–34), emotions that Matthew and Luke tone down in their respective tellings. Mark's Jesus is fiery when the situation demands, and his call to follow him is uncompromising and insistent. He becomes exasperated at times with the "hard-heartedness"—i.e., lack of comprehension—that his disciples exhibit more than once. Throughout the Gospel there is a pressing sense of urgency. Something startlingly new has appeared: the kingdom of God is being revealed and the time has come for "repentance"—meaning, literally, the transformation of one's thoughts, mind, heart: an *inner* transfiguration that is manifested in one's actions and behavior. It's no accident that Jesus is "transfigured" (μετεμορφώθη) midway through the Gospel; it lies—along with Peter's confession that Jesus is the Christ—at the heart of the narrative. It is the center of the text's overall chiastic ("X") shape, as mentioned in the previous chapter, which indicates its importance within the story. It's *there* that *who* Jesus is and what it is towards which he summons his disciples is unsettlingly glimpsed.

Here is what I regard to be the *basic* three-section outline of Mark's Gospel. It is a simplification of a more elaborate summary of the contents of the book. Others sometimes list as many as five sections, but whether Mark is divided into three or five segments, the central portion is always suggestively the same. My three-section outline is as follows:

1. Chapters 1:1–8:21: Jesus proclaims the kingdom of God by word and deed, first in Galilee and then beyond to both Jews and gentiles.

2. Chapters 8:22–10:52: Jesus reveals himself by stages to his disciples (culminating in the Transfiguration) and begins his journey to Jerusalem; this section—a chiasm—is sandwiched between two transitional stories in which Jesus heals persons afflicted with blindness (note: as we will see, there is significance in the fact that the first healing of a blind man is *gradual*, while the second such healing is *immediate* in its effect).

3. Chapters 11:1–16:8: Jesus comes to Jerusalem, is betrayed, crucified, and resurrects.

With that in mind, we will look more closely at the "mystical" aspects of Mark. Keep in mind what lies at the heart of the Gospel narrative (the Transfiguration account), and along with it look ahead to what Paul says in 2 Corinthians 3:18 and 4:6.

2.

The Gospel of Mark commences and concludes abruptly, which has led many scholars to believe that the original beginning and ending of the book were lost early on. This is certainly plausible (and is the view I hold), given that the manuscript of Mark was a codex and not a scroll. A codex is a book inscribed on sheets of papyrus or vellum, folded, and sewn down the middle, forming pages to be read as we still read books today. If early in the text's existence the outer sheet(s) had somehow become unloosed from the body of the book — torn off, perhaps — it's a simple inference to think that both "ends" of the text went missing.

There are scholars, on the other hand, who argue that we have Mark in its entirety, that nothing was lost, and that the author intended for it to begin with Jesus's baptism and finish with the women hastening away in fear from the tomb and not saying a word to anybody — just as we have it. There is no way we can know for sure, of course, which theory (or whether either of them) is correct. As I said, I tend to believe that the text is missing its opening and concluding portions. I suspect that Mark originally did have both a birth narrative and resurrection appearances, like the other two Synoptics. In 14:28, in the context of the Last Supper, Jesus tells his disciples, "But after I am raised up, I will go before you to Galilee." This could very well suggest that Mark's Gospel originally ended with a post-resurrection appearance set in Galilee, as we have it in Matthew's Gospel. I find this possibility more likely than not.

Still, there is some meager evidence that *maybe* Mark ended the Gospel as we have it in order to draw a

comparison between Jesus and the Old Testament patriarch, Joseph. The final sentence in Mark is 16:8. Additional endings, which still appear in our Bibles, were
(rather clumsily) added later. Here is 16:8, and pay particular attention to the final Greek word in it:

καὶ ἐξελθοῦσαι ἔφυγον ἀπὸ τοῦ μνημείου, εἶχεν γὰρ αὐτὰς
τρόμος καὶ ἔκστασις: καὶ οὐδενὶ οὐδὲν εἶπαν, ἐφοβοῦντο γάρ
(And going out, they fled from the tomb, for trembling and bewilderment had taken hold of them; and
they said nothing to anyone; for they were afraid; or,
literally, "they were afraid for.")

What is striking about this sentence is that it ends with
the word γάρ ("*gar*")—which literally means "for." Such
an ending for a sentence in Greek is certainly not without
precedent. There is a text in Genesis concerning Joseph,
as I mentioned, which has a similar construction, and it
might be relevant. If so, it could indicate that we have the
Gospel's final sentence as Mark originally wrote it. It's a
long shot (much too long for me to find it convincing),
but in the Greek version of the Hebrew scriptures that
early Christians tended to use (the Septuagint, designated
by the Roman numeral LXX), this sentence structure
shows up in Genesis 45:3. It occurs in a scene that in some
respects resembles Mark 16:8 not only in grammar but
also in content. The moment described is that wherein
Joseph *reveals himself to be alive* to his brothers: καὶ οὐκ
ἠδύναντο οἱ ἀδελφοὶ ἀποκριθῆναι αὐτῷ· ἐταράχθησαν γάρ
("and his brothers could not answer him, for they were
troubled"—literally, "they were troubled for"). Note
that the sentence, like Mark 16:8, ends with γάρ, "for."
This poses a provocative but unanswerable question for
us: Is Mark 16:8 connecting the revelation that *Jesus is
alive* to the women at the tomb with Joseph revealing
to his brothers that *he is alive*? It's an intriguing thought
if nothing more.

There are two other features in Mark that I wish to
explore here and in the following section of this chapter.

The first of these is the question of what lies at the core
of the Gospel, because, as we have noted already, what
is *central* to the text provides us with an interpretive key
to the rest. The second, which we will look at in the next
section, has to do with a peculiar literary device that
connects Jesus's arrest in Gethsemane with the revelation
to the women at the tomb. Both features build on other
features in the Gospel, as we will note, and—more to
the point—they reflect the presumed mystical tradition
that shaped the Gospel.

As you will recall, in the previous section I broke the
Gospel into three large portions as follows. Here I want
to concentrate on verses 8:22–10:52, in which Jesus reveals
himself gradually to his disciples and sets out on his
journey to Jerusalem. As we noted, this portion of Mark
is sandwiched between two stories that tell about Jesus
healing blind men.

Before we look at that central block of the text, it's
important to take note of what takes place in the narrative that precedes it. To summarize, in the first eight
chapters, Jesus has called his disciples to follow him, has
confronted opponents among the Pharisees, has taught
his followers "in parables," and has performed a series
of increasingly astounding wonders—curing a demoniac,
then "many" at Simon Peter's house, including Peter's
mother-in-law, a leper, a paralytic, a man with a withered
hand, and many among a crowd at the seaside; he silences
a storm, exorcises a demoniac in gentile territory who is
possessed by a "legion" of unclean spirits, raises to life a
dead girl and heals a woman with a flow of blood, feeds
five thousand with five loaves and two fish, heals many in
a crowd in Gennesaret, cures a gentile woman's daughter
at a distance, heals a deaf man, and feeds four thousand
with seven loaves and a few small fishes.

There can be little doubt that Jesus was a healer and
performed what John's Gospel explicitly calls "signs."
And here we need to pause and reflect on that designation.

That his works are "signs" indicates that they invite interpretation: this is made clear, for example, in the account of the healing of the paralytic, where Jesus says to the consternation of the Pharisees who question his ability to forgive sins (which, in their understanding, was a strictly divine prerogative):

> "Which is easier, to say to the paralytic, 'Your sins are forgiven,' or to say, 'Rise and take up your pallet and walk'? But in order that you should know that the Son of Man [a phrase used for the Messiah] has power to forgive sins on the earth..." [He says to the paralytic] "I say to you, rise, take up your pallet, and go to your house." (2:9–11)

In the spiritual sense of the text, then, paralysis is a symbol for what sins do to a person. They inwardly "paralyze" a person, requiring a salvific act of forgiveness. The paralytic's "raising up" suggests a sort of resurrection out of a state of deadness. This is not to say that physical ailments are the consequence of sins committed, but that the physical conditions that Jesus cures in the Gospel stories are signs and symbols of spiritual maladies that cry out for healing. There's more going on in the stories of Jesus curing, say, a leper or a deaf man than the physical healings themselves.

Likewise, with his signs of power—Jesus's calming of the storm, walking on the water, multiplying loaves and fishes (performed *twice*—a significant number, as we will see below), and so on—are more than accounts of literal "nature miracles." Something much more profound is being indicated. I will only mention in passing that stories involving water have baptismal connotations and the feeding accounts point toward a Eucharistic interpretation within the Petrine-Pauline tradition; Paul, writing about two decades before the composition of Mark, even reads the Hebrew Bible with these analogies in mind, for example, in 1 Corinthians 10:1–4. The spiritual sense of Jesus's miraculous signs becomes explicitly evident when we turn to the passage in which Jesus's disciples misunderstand his words about "the yeast of the Pharisees and the yeast of Herod" (8:13–21). And it's this passage — take note — that *immediately* precedes and sets us up for the central section of the Gospel.

Here is the passage:

> And he left [the Pharisees who demanded from him a sign], and getting into the boat again he departed to the other side. Now [the disciples] had forgotten to bring bread; and they had only one loaf with them in the boat. And he cautioned them, saying, "Take heed, beware of the leaven of the Pharisees and the leaven of Herod." And they discussed it with one another, saying, "We have no bread." And being aware of it, Jesus said to them, "Why do you discuss the fact that you have no bread? Do you not yet perceive or understand? Are your hearts hardened? Having eyes do you not see, and having ears do you not hear? And do you not remember? When I broke the five loaves for the five thousand, how many baskets full of broken pieces did you take up?" They said to him, "Twelve." "And the seven for the four thousand, how many baskets full of broken pieces did you take up?" And they said to him, "Seven." And he said to them, "Do you not yet understand?"

Like the outsiders mentioned in 4:10–12, who cannot understand his parables, the disciples lack understanding: their hearts are "hardened." Having eyes and ears, they don't see or hear what Jesus is revealing. More to the point — and frequently overlooked by commentators — Jesus expects the disciples to understand the significance of the *numbers* involved in the two feeding accounts: five, five thousand, twelve; seven, four thousand, seven. He, in fact, stresses those numbers and remarks on his closest followers' incomprehension concerning what they "add up to." He is not, as is often supposed, merely pointing to how much abundance he had created from next to nothing. He very specifically demands that they *understand* the *precise numbers* involved in the miracles, which they are able to recall quite clearly.

We can, at this distance, only guess what the numbers might signify. Perhaps the most plausible explanation is that the feeding of the five thousand represents an abundant provision to the Israelite people. The sign occurs in a desert region and those present are Hebrews, just like their forebears who had wandered in the desert under Moses's leadership. The numbers five and five thousand are suggestive of the five books of the Law and the bread is evocative of the manna in the desert. The number twelve is reminiscent of the twelve tribes. On the other hand, the feeding of the four thousand appears to occur somewhere in the region of the Decapolis (the "Ten Cities"), a region with a notable gentile population (see 7:31). If that can be safely assumed, then the number seven might be suggestive of the "seventy nations of the world," and the four thousand might indicate a thousand (a symbolic number for "many") gathered from each of the four corners of the earth. In other words, what Jesus provides in his miracles of feeding is for both the children of Israel and the gentiles. If that interpretation strikes us as too fanciful, it wouldn't necessarily have struck the first-century Jewish and gentile Christians in Rome — those for whom Mark's Gospel was written, in other words — that way at all. Once again, we need to read these texts, as best we can, through the lens of the tradition of the community that first read them.

The message to those early Christian readers, then, would have been: "Open your own eyes and ears and pay attention to these accounts. They have meaning *for you*, whatever your background or ethnicity." But no matter how we interpret the numerology in the passage, it is *this* story that sets us up for the central section of Mark. And the transitional story into that section is, very significantly indeed, all about *a healing of blindness* — and not *just* a healing of blindness but an unusually *gradual* healing at that. Further, what we are about to witness in 8:22–10:52 is a *gradual* opening of the disciples' inner eyes — and that, of course, was implicitly just as pointed an expectation for the Gospel's readers as for the apostles in the account.

The healing of the blind man in 8:22–26 comes in three stages. Jesus spits into the man's eyes, lays his hands on him, and inquires, "Do you see anything?" The man replies that he is beginning to see, but at first, he sees only blurred images: "I see men; but they look like trees, walking." This is stage one of his healing. Again, Jesus lays hands on him, and the man "looked intently" — this is the second stage — "and he was restored, and he saw everything clearly" — the third stage. Then Jesus says to him that he should not publicly advertise the fact of his sight's restoration.

Immediately following this passage is the account of Jesus and his disciples — the same men he had just chided for their hardness of heart in not *seeing* or *hearing* what he had revealed to them thus far — going into Caesarea Philippi. There he will ask them pointedly who "the people" are saying he is, and then, even more pointedly, who *they* believe him to be. Peter declares, "You are the Christ [the Anointed One]." And immediately, Jesus warns them, as he had warned the formerly blind man in the previous passage to keep quiet, to "tell no one about him."

In other words, Jesus is about to "open the eyes" of his disciples *in stages*:

In 8:31, he proceeds to give the first of *three* teachings about his coming death and resurrection. These three dire teachings (the other two are found in 9:30–32 and 10:32–34) *progressively* become more detailed. As with the blind man's three-stage healing, so the predictions concerning his sufferings come in three stages. Nor should we ignore that, overall, the revelation to the disciples of his identity and work comes in this Gospel in *three* stages, in other words, in the three divisions of the Gospel itself. In chapters 1 through 8, his disciples saw things "blurred," "like trees, walking"; in this section, his disciples will be forced to "look intently" and—as we will see in the Transfiguration account—"listen [only] to him." Before he gives the final prediction of his coming Passion in 10:32–34, his followers will be just beginning to realize the import of what he has been telling them: "And they were on the road [a significant phrase—being "on the road" suggests "following Jesus in the way" and "bearing after him one's cross"], going up to Jerusalem [where he will die], and Jesus was walking ahead of them; and they were amazed, and those who followed were afraid" (10:32). In other words, by this point, it's starting to sink in that something horribly troubling is about to happen, and they're perplexed.

But that's not all. The final section of the Gospel is preceded by *another* healing of blindness. This time, though, the healing is immediate; and the passage concludes—again, very significantly—with these words: "immediately [the healed man] received his sight and *followed him on the way*" (10:52; emphasis added). This *enlightened* man, who can now *see clearly*, is a model of discipleship. That's the spiritual significance of his "following" Jesus "on the way" (i.e., to the cross).

To return to the exchange between Jesus and the twelve at Caesarea Philippi, after he foretold what would befall him in Jerusalem, Peter—who had just pronounced him "the Christ"—"took hold of him" and admonished him. Jesus, in turn, rebuked Peter harshly, "Get behind me, Satan! For you are not on the side of God, but of men" (8:33). He then speaks the crucial words to his disciples and the gathered crowd—and by extension, the readers of the Gospel—"If any man would come after me, let him deny himself and take up his cross and follow me" (10:34). As noted, this is what the second blind man represents when he "follows" Jesus on "the way" to Jerusalem. Jesus's discourse concludes in 9:1, where he says, "Truly, I say to you, there are some standing here who will not taste death before they see that the kingdom of God has come with power." This is *not* a reference to the coming of the kingdom of God at the end of the age, but to that event that three of his disciples—Peter, James, and John—will be privileged to behold on the mount, the Transfiguration.

Here is the beating heart of Mark's Gospel. As the narrative unfolded, those who listened to this account read aloud in those early Roman gatherings would have known "who Jesus is" before he endured the cross and Passion. The Father, after all, had declared it to Jesus at his baptism in what would become the text of the first chapter, and even the demons he exorcised had known his identity. When Jesus, then, asks his disciples, "Who do you say that I am?" he's *not* trying to figure out his identity nor seeking their opinion on the matter (as has, rather inexplicably, been suggested by some "exegetes"). He quite clearly knows who he is and where it is that he's headed. Not only that, but the readers of the Gospel know it, too: along with the disciples with whom the readers are meant to identify, they know that the disclosure of Jesus's identity comes in stages. It won't fully be disclosed, though, until the revelation of the empty tomb. But, before we reach that moment of ultimate truth, it's the Transfiguration scene that really brings everything together in this Gospel, particularly with the Father's second declaration about the Son: "This is my beloved Son; *listen to him*" (9:7; emphasis added).

There's no need here to quote the full passage; I leave it to you to read over Mark's version for yourself (and perhaps compare it to Matthew's and Luke's versions, which have some notable variations). All that should be noted here is that it's presented as a revelation of "the kingdom of God come in power" and thus, as intimately related to the coming resurrection: "And as they were coming down the mountain, [Jesus] charged them to tell no one what they had seen, until the Son of man

should have risen from the dead" (9:9) — a warning
that provokes the three disciples to debate what "rising
from the dead" means. The Transfiguration account is
as close as we have to a resurrection appearance in the
Gospel of Mark (which, as I noted earlier, appears to be
incomplete). What Mark is saying is that Jesus's identity,
as revealed in his unveiled glory on the mountain, is
what makes his victory over death and the grave inevi-
table — his life *cannot* be swallowed up by death, despite
his obvious flesh and blood humanity.

The audience that first heard this Gospel read in their
gatherings understood the mystical import of all this,
and they identified themselves with the disciples in the
text who were learning by stages ("from glory to glory";
2 Cor. 3:18). The meaning for them was directly related
to their union with Christ in baptism and in their celebration of the Eucharistic mystery. The book was for
their contemplation, communally and individually. It
fed their faith and informed their actions. As believers
in the Petrine-Pauline gospel, they already understood
that Jesus's Transfiguration was intimately related to their
own transformation into his image. These Christians
saw themselves, as 2 Peter 1:4 puts it, as "communicants
in the divine nature" — an epistolary chapter that also
includes a direct reference to the Transfiguration of Jesus
(2 Peter 1:17–18). This was the heart of the tradition: their
share in the glorification of Jesus — what would later be
called "deification" in the great Tradition.

3.

In the Gospel of Mark, the Transfiguration scene *illu-
minates* everything that precedes the event and everything
that follows. This is not the case in the other three Gospels, as we will see when we discuss those texts. If earlier
in the Gospel, Jesus could accuse the disciples of obduracy
of heart — neither seeing nor listening nor remembering what he had revealed to them — with this event the

privileged trio of Peter, James, and John had their eyes
and ears opened in a stunning way. They were ushered
without warning into the presence of the glory that had
descended in former times on the Tabernacle and the
Temple, but here it shone from their Master. Through
the person of Jesus, in other words, they perceived the
radiance of divinity. It was the hitherto unseen power,
abiding in Christ, that could heal with a touch, raise
the dead, expel evil, and — as the resurrection would
reveal — not be overcome by death. In essence, this is
the defining moment of the book and a revelation of the
transcendent life in which the Gospel's readers partici-
pated as "communicants in the divine nature" (2 Pet. 1:4).

In light of the Transfiguration, too, the basis for what
has been termed the "messianic secret" is made evident.
Jesus wasn't merely being "secretive" about himself when
he, for example, had "warned [the disciples] sternly that
they should tell no one about him," following Peter's confession that he was the Messiah (8:30), or when, after the
Transfiguration, he exhorted Peter, James, and John not
to relate what they had seen until after his resurrection
(9:9). He was warning them not to talk about *what they
could not yet fully understand* but would come to realize
after he rose from the dead.

Earlier, I described very briefly the communal and
conceptual context in which the Gospels were written.
The most important aspect to recall is that the early
Christians understood themselves *to have been united to
Christ's death and resurrection* through the Spirit ("Breath"
or creative "Wind") of God, through the mystery of
baptism "into Christ." Even their physical bodies were
members of his Body, and Christ's indestructible life
now coursed through them. Again and again throughout
the New Testament, this idea that "his life is mine" and
that our true lives are already "risen with Christ" and
"hidden in him" is declared openly as the basis for every
other aspect of Christian existence. Comparatively, one's

culture, status, family identity, ethnicity, wealth, and so on are merely passing and trivial, and will pass away entirely when either we or this age expires (whichever comes first): "What we shall be does not yet appear" (1 John 3:2). When early Christians, then, read about the Transfiguration, they recognized that the glorious life revealed in it was—in seed form and burgeoning—at work within them. This was the reality in which they were communicants. This was the new life into which they had been immersed in baptism.

That baptism is another key to interpreting the Gospel of Mark seems to be evident in one of the more obscure characters, who appears only (and literally) fleetingly in the text—and he appears only in Mark's Gospel. I have sometimes suspected that this character is a literary device (the Evangelists were not averse to employing literary devices; for example, as we will see when we come to Matthew's Gospel, the author uses the device of "doubling" characters and even animals suggestively). We will come to him in due course, but before we do, and in order to make sense of his brief appearance, we must note a few details about how baptism was performed in the early churches.

The primary sources we have (the *Didache, The Apostolic Tradition* attributed to Hippolytus of Rome, the *Mystagogical Catecheses* of Cyril of Jerusalem, and so on) outline common practices that probably date from the earliest period of the church, and thus give us some insight into what may have been the custom in the churches that read Mark's Gospel. *The Apostolic Tradition* (c. 215) describes the baptismal procedure in this way:

> Those who are to receive baptism shall fast on the Preparation of the Sabbath. On the Sabbath, those who are to receive baptism shall all gather together in one place chosen according to the will of the bishop. They shall be commanded to pray and kneel. Then, laying his hand on them, he will exorcise every foreign spirit, so that they flee from them and never return

to them. When he has finished exorcising them, he shall breathe on their faces and seal their foreheads, ears and noses. Then he shall raise them up.

They shall all keep vigil all night, reading and instructing them.

Those who are to be baptized are not to bring any vessel, only that which each brings for the eucharist. It is indeed proper that each bring the oblation in the same hour.

At the hour in which the cock crows, they shall first pray over the water. When they come to the water, the water shall be pure and flowing, that is, the water of a spring or a flowing body of water. *Then they shall take off all their clothes.* The children shall be baptized first. All of the children who can answer for themselves, let them answer. If there are any children who cannot answer for themselves, let their parents answer for them, or someone else from their family. After this, the men will be baptized. Finally, the women, after they have unbound their hair, and removed their jewelry. No one shall take any foreign object with themselves down into the water.

At the time determined for baptism, the bishop shall give thanks over some oil, which he puts in a vessel. It is called the Oil of Thanksgiving. He shall take some more oil and exorcise it. It is called the Oil of Exorcism. A deacon shall hold the Oil of Exorcism and stand on the left. Another deacon shall hold the Oil of Thanksgiving and stand on the right.

When the elder takes hold of each of them who are to receive baptism, he shall tell each of them to renounce, saying, "I renounce you Satan, all your service, and all your works."

After he has said this, he shall anoint each with the Oil of Exorcism, saying, "Let every evil spirit depart from you." Then, after these things, *the bishop passes each of them on nude to the elder* who stands at the water. *They shall stand in the water naked.* A deacon, likewise, will go down with them into the water. When each of them to be baptized has gone down into the water, the one baptizing shall lay hands on each of them, asking, "Do you believe in God the Father Almighty?" And the one being baptized shall answer, "I believe." He shall then baptize each of them once, laying his hand upon each of their heads. Then he shall ask, "Do you believe in Jesus Christ, the Son of God, who was born of the Holy Spirit and the Virgin Mary, who was crucified under Pontius Pilate, and died, and rose on the third day living from the dead, and ascended into heaven, and sat down at the right hand of the Father, the one coming to judge the living and the dead?" When each has answered, "I believe," he shall baptize a second time. Then he shall ask, "Do you believe in the Holy Spirit and the Holy Church and the resurrection of the flesh?" Then each being baptized shall answer, "I believe." And thus let him baptize the third time.

Afterward, when they have come up out of the water, they shall be anointed by the elder with the Oil of Thanksgiving, saying, "I anoint you with holy oil in the name of Jesus Christ." Then, drying themselves, *they shall dress* and afterwards gather in the church.[4]

Note the italicized sentences and phrases above, and especially these three stages of the baptismal rites: (1) There is an all-night vigil, during which the baptizands are given their *final teachings* (through readings and oral instruction); (2) the baptizands *strip themselves of their clothing* and are baptized *naked*; (3) they are *re-clothed* and gather in the place of worship. About a century and a half after Hippolytus, we find Cyril of Jerusalem describing similar rites, along with explanations of what they signify:

> As soon, therefore, as ye entered [into the inner chamber], *ye put off your garment*; and this was an image of *putting off the old man with his deeds* [Col. 3:9; italics original]. *Having stripped yourselves, ye were naked; in*

---

[4] *The Apostolic Tradition*, 20.7–21.20; emphasis added. This translation can be found at: https://www.stjohnsarlingtonva.org/Customer-Content/saintjohnsarlington/CMS/files/EFM/Apostolic_Tradition_by_Hippolytus.pdf.

this also imitating Christ, who hung naked on the cross, and
by His nakedness *spoiled principalities and powers and
openly triumphed over them on the tree* [Col. 2:15; italics
original]. For since the powers of the enemy made
their lair in your members, ye may no longer wear
that old vestment; I do not at all mean this visible
one, but *that old man, which is corrupt according to the
deceitful lusts* [Eph. 4:22] . . .

But now, *having put off thy old garments, and put on
those which are spiritually white,* thou must be continually
robed in white; we mean not this, that thou must
always wear white raiment; but with truly white and
glistering and spiritual attire, thou must be clothed
withal, that thou mayest say with the blessed Esaias,
*My soul shall be joyful in my God; for He hath clothed me
with the garments of salvation, He hath covered me with the
robe of gladness* [Isa. 61:10, LXX].[5]

Once again, the stripping off of garments, baptism in
the nude, and the re-clothing afterwards have significance — and Cyril's full text is far richer in explaining
the symbolism than the two snippets above indicate.

Returning to the Gospel of Mark, we find these same
symbols or "stages" in relation to a mysterious figure
who — again, quite literally — flits through the narrative
at an important moment and who will reappear in the
Gospel in a later scene. I refer to the "young man" (νεανί-
σκος, "*neaniskos*") who is mentioned in 14:51–52, as the
disciples flee in the wake of Jesus's arrest in Gethsemane,
and who turns up once more in 16:5–7 to announce to
the women that Jesus has risen from the dead.

The *neaniskos* first appears suddenly in the narrative.
There he is stripped of his garment, and flees along with
the (other) disciples: "And a young man followed him,
with nothing but a linen cloth about his body; and they
seized him, but he left the linen cloth and ran away

---

[5] Cyril of Jerusalem, *Mystagogical Catecheses*, II.2; IV.8, in *Lectures
on the Christian Sacraments*, ed. F. L. Cross (Crestwood, 1977), 59,
70. Unless otherwise noted, emphasis mine.

naked." We should note that he is described as "following" Christ. As with the blind man whom Jesus healed in Chapter 10 and who "followed him on the way" afterwards, this young man is a "follower," that is to say, a disciple. We would probably be mistaken to try to assign to him a specific historical identity (such as John Mark, the author of the Gospel). Assuming — as I do — that he is to be identified with the *neaniskos* who appears at the empty tomb later, we would likely be correct to regard him as a "type," a figure who is best interpreted allegorically. Without belaboring the point, he likely represents the baptized follower of Jesus: first, he is stripped of his garments (as Jesus will be at his humiliation and crucifixion, and as baptizands will be before their baptism), he flees along with the other disciples, but he reappears as a witness to Jesus's resurrection, *re-clothed*: "And entering the tomb [the women] saw a young man sitting to the right [perhaps a significant placement; Jesus sits "at the right hand of the Father"], *clothed in a white robe*, and they were amazed" (16:5; emphasis added). He represents the *reborn disciple*, identified with Jesus both in his death and in his resurrection; in other words, he represents precisely what the mystery of baptism effects in the believer. He is risen with Christ and "hidden in" (meaning "united with") Christ, who is "sitting at God's right hand" (see Col. 3:1–4). To link this, then, to what was revealed in the Transfiguration, the disciple has come to realize in himself the divine life that Jesus revealed in that event. He is now, as by a gift bestowed, a communicant in this same divine nature. For him, death is no longer something to be feared — he has already "died": "by baptism into death we were buried with [Jesus]" (Rom. 6:4).

There is a third text that mentions the "young man," which in all likelihood was later added to the text of Mark in Alexandria. The text is known as the "Secret Gospel of Mark." It has, at best, a spotty reputation (it is quite possibly a modern forgery). But, fraudulent or not, it

appears to be a version of the raising of Lazarus, which
we know from John 11. The most important fragment
(of two) is this:

> And they come into Bethany. And a certain woman
> whose brother had died was there. And, coming, she
> prostrated herself before Jesus and says to him, "Son of
> David, have mercy on me." But the disciples rebuked
> her. And Jesus, being angered, went off with her into
> the garden where the tomb was, and straightway a
> great cry was heard from the tomb. And going near
> Jesus rolled away the stone from the door of the tomb.
> And straightway, going in where the young man [*nean-
> iskos*] was, he stretched forth his hand and raised him,
> seizing his hand. But the young man, looking upon
> him, loved him and began to beseech him that he
> might be with him. And going out of the tomb they
> came into the house of the young man, for he was rich.
> And after six days Jesus told him what to do and, in
> the evening, the young man comes to him, wearing
> a linen cloth over his naked body. And he remained
> with him that night, for Jesus taught him the mys-
> tery of the kingdom of God. And thence, arising, he
> returned to the other side of the Jordan.

Whether or not this passage really is a "lost" part of
the original Gospel, we will probably never know. The
fact that it was purportedly found in a letter of Clement
of Alexandria, the genuineness of which is likewise up
for grabs (rather suspiciously, it has gone missing since
its "discovery"), and appears in no ancient text of Mark,
suggests strongly that it isn't original. At most, it's a curi-
osity. The takeaway is that, once again, we have the young
man associated with death and resurrection. He seeks
to follow Jesus and goes through a period of instruction
at night—in effect, a pre-baptismal vigil, such as that
described in *The Apostolic Tradition* of Hippolytus above.
If it's genuine, it merely reinforces the interpretation that
the figure of the *neaniskos* is representative of discipleship
and the central Christian mystery.

To conclude these notes on Mark's Gospel, before turning our attention to Matthew's, we can say that this Gospel, as short and "punchy" as it is, is nonetheless spiritually rich. There is far more to it than appears on its rough, choppy surface. For the prayerful, contemplative reader, no "deep dive" can ever reach its bottommost depth, but it will always have more to give us with each reading. It may be the shortest of the Gospels, but by no means can it be said to be shallow.

III

The Gospel of Matthew

1.

An image of Jesus we see repeatedly portrayed in first-world contexts — be it in sermons, books, inspirational memes on social media, or in film and TV — is one that tends to soothe and "affirm" us just as we are. This Jesus never makes demands on us; he accepts us without any expectation that we should alter our thinking; he isn't a "lawgiver" and never mentions anything as unpleasant as judgment; all his teachings are reducible to a plea that we be more "loving" (I'm tempted to say "nice"). He's also given to smiling a lot and generally behaving like the sort of friendly neighbor who wants to be a pal. Of course, this sort of misrepresentation of Christ (and others equally mawkish) is matched by the harsh misrepresentations of fundamentalist Christians. Both are distortions, with no support from the original Tradition.

When we turn to the Gospel of Matthew, we haven't any choice but to encounter there a Jesus who *does* make demands, who is *not* opposed to law and, in fact, *is* a lawgiver. The Christ we find in Matthew expects from his hearers a change of heart, and — to the dismay of some first-time, first-world readers, no doubt — he speaks about judgment frequently. Indeed, in this Gospel we encounter Jesus as Master, the Son who knows and can alone reveal the Father to the world (11:27), whose body of teachings concludes with a parable that tells us unequivocally that our lives and actions are ultimately destined to be taken seriously (25:31–46). Contemporary sentiments will need to be set aside if we want to understand Christ as presented to us by Matthew (and, of course, the same applies to all the Gospels).

At the center of the Gospel of Mark, as we proposed, was the Transfiguration of Jesus. That event provided the interpretive key to Mark. The Transfiguration revealed the "divine nature" in which Christ's followers were to become "communicants" (see 2 Pet. 1:4) and into which gradually—"from glory to glory"—they were themselves being inwardly transfigured (see 2 Cor. 3:18). In the figure of the "young man" of 14:51–52 and 16:5, who stands in Mark as a "type" of the disciple, they could recognize an allusion to the stripping away of the old life and re-clothing in the new life through their baptism into the death and resurrection of Jesus. Mark, as we said, was written within what can broadly be called the "Petrine-Pauline" tradition—the tradition, in fact, that underlies the entire New Testament canon.

The Tradition of the church has always affirmed that Mark's Gospel was "the preaching of Peter" as committed to writing by Mark. In that sense, it was recognized as decidedly "Petrine." Mark certainly doesn't disparage the person of Peter in any way, but it can't be said to be "Petrine" in an acclamatory way, either. Note, for instance, its treatment of Peter's confession that Jesus is "the Christ," which is immediately followed by a command to keep quiet about the claim and, a few verses later, comes Jesus's startlingly stern rebuke of Peter: "Get behind me, Satan! For you are not on the side of God, but of men" (Mark 8:29–33). Peter receives no great credit for his insight regarding Jesus's identity. Contrast this treatment of Peter by Jesus in Mark's account with how Matthew presents the same story: there, although the later rebuke is also included, Peter is given Jesus's blessing, nicknamed "the Rock," and given the "keys" as the church's future chief rabbi (Matt. 16:15–19[1]). There can be little doubt that Matthew stands at the "Petrine" end of the Tradition in his high regard for that apostle. So, then, what is the telltale "center" of Matthew's

---

[1] Compare verse 19 with Isaiah 22:20–22.

Gospel—its interpretive key, in other words? It is not the Transfiguration, as in Mark, but rather, Jesus's first round of parables in Chapter 13.

My intention, as I look at Matthew's Gospel, is to explore as briefly as possible *five* features that will help us to recognize its distinctiveness among the four. As we know, each of the Gospels has a perspective all its own; no two are identical. And—despite much later doctrinal assertions regarding the non-contradictory nature of biblical texts—their accounts even of the same episodes often differ in numerous details. This will become strikingly apparent, for instance, as we compare Matthew's tendency to "double" both persons and even animals whereas Mark and Luke only have single individuals in their versions of the very same stories. It's even evident in the Transfiguration scene, in which Mark prioritizes the appearance of Elijah over Moses ("there appeared to them Elijah with Moses"; Mark 9:4),[2] while both Matthew (for reasons that will become clearer as we look at the centrality of the Mosaic Law in this Gospel) and Luke do precisely the opposite, both mentioning Moses before Elijah. The differences between versions of the same or similar accounts in the Gospels do not seem to have bothered early Christian readers and exegetes; they saw in the discrepancies the work of divine inspiration, providing them with a variety of complementary insights. And while there have always been those who wished to blend the four texts in a single, non-contradictory porridge (beginning as early as Tatian's *Diatessaron* in the second century), the church very wisely opted to keep its four Gospels *distinct*.

Turning to the preliminaries, scholarship has tended to date Matthew's Gospel to sometime in the 80s, although some would put it earlier and some later. There are

---

[2] The priority of Elijah is stressed in Mark 9 possibly because the identification of that ancient prophet's promised return with the ministry of John the Baptist is discussed by Jesus and the three disciples immediately after the Transfiguration.

indications in the Gospel that the Temple had been destroyed by the time of its writing (see 12:6; 22:7). Its place of origin is thought to be the region of Antioch in Syria. Only Matthew among the Gospels mentions Syria (4:24). Ignatius of Antioch, whose epistles date to circa 110, seems to have been aware of traditions and expressions found in Matthew (*Smyrneans* 1:1; 6:1; *Trallians* 11:1; *Philadelphians* 3:1; *Polycarp* 2:2; etc.). The Gospel's author is traditionally said to have been Matthew, the tax collector Jesus called to be his disciple (9:9–13). Matthew's Gospel is the only one to call him by this name; both Mark and Luke refer to him as "Levi" (see Mark 2:13–17; Luke 5:27–28). It has been argued, plausibly or not, that this indicates that Matthew possibly preferred to be known by this name. It has also been said that the saying of Jesus, found only in Matthew's Gospel, that "every scribe who has been made a disciple to the Kingdom of the heavens is like a man who is master of a house, who brings forth things new and old from his treasury" (Matt. 13:52) is the author showing his hand. He is the Evangelist who more often than the rest quotes from the Old Testament.

There are five distinguishing features of Matthew that I will concentrate on. Through them, we should become more alert to the contours and content of the book.

1. The Gospel of Matthew contains *five major discourses* of Jesus.

2. It is the *third discourse* — made up of Jesus's first series of parables (13:1–53) — that is at the center of the Gospel's chiastic structure. As we will see, it is this section that provides an interpretive key for the rest of the book.

3. The *progression of parables* throughout Matthew, from the parable of the sower and the seed (13:3–23) to that of the judgment of the "nations" (ἔθνη, "*ethne*," 25:31–46; this judgment is of the same "*ethne*" that are referred to in 28:19, meaning those who have heard the apostles' teaching) is important for understanding the overall message of the book.

4. The *strained relations* between Matthew's *ekklesia* and other Jewish communities are implicit in the text. Part of the strain between these different communities, both sprung from a common Hebrew root, may have been the result of the acceptance of uncircumcised gentiles as members of the Christian church in Antioch, a feature explicitly on exhibit in Paul's Letter to the Galatians and in the book of Acts. Consequently, the theme of the inclusion of gentiles is an important one for Matthew. This Gospel is concerned with affirming both a firm adherence to the faith of Israel and the church's mission to the "nations" ("gentiles").

5. *Matthew is given to doubling,* as we noted in passing above. There are *two* demoniacs in Matthew 8:28–34, instead of just one in Mark 5:1–17 and Luke 8:26–39; *two* blind men in Matthew 9:27–31, and *two* more blind men in 20:29–34 (compare Mark 8:22–26; 10:46–52; Luke 18:35–43); and Jesus (somehow) rides into Jerusalem on an ass *and* a foal — *two* animals — in Matthew 21:1–11, rather than on the single animal of Mark 11:1–11 and Luke 19:29–38. This should clue us in to the fact that there is undoubtedly a spiritual sense to be derived from this doubling tendency, which we will explore in due course. It relates, I will suggest, to an important theme that we have already noted.

Looking at the first of the five features above, then, the Gospel of Matthew presents us with *five major discourses* of Jesus. As we saw when we dealt with the feeding of the five thousand in the Gospel of Mark, the number five has significance in Hebrew numerology. Most importantly, there are five books of the Torah.[3] This may be what underlies the significance of Jesus's *five* discourses, all five of which are given for the sake of establishing his *ekklesia* ("assembly"; translated as "church"). The word *ekklesia* is used throughout the Septuagint (LXX), but

---

[3] There are, possibly relatedly, five divisions in the Psalter: 1–41, 42–72, 73–89, 90–106, 107–50.

most notably to designate the Israelites who followed Moses in the Exodus (e.g., Deut. 4:10; 9:10; 18:16; 31:30). Before coming back to this theme, here is the outline of Matthew's Gospel, the central portion of which revolves around Jesus's five discourses:

I. Prologue: The Infancy Narrative (chap. 1 and 2)

Middle Portion:

II. Section 1 (chap. 3–7)Narrative (chap. 3 and 4)
Discourse: The Sermon on the Mount (chap. 5–7)
"... *when Jesus completed these sayings*... " (7:28)

III. Section 2 (chaps. 8–11:1)
Narrative (chaps. 8:1–9:34)
Discourse: The Mission Directives (9:35–11:1)
"... *when Jesus completed these sayings*... " (11:1)

IV. Section 3 (11:2–13:52)
Narrative (11:2–12:50)
Discourse: The First Round of Parables (13:1–53)
"... *when Jesus completed these sayings*... " (13:53)

V. Section 4 (13:54–18:35)
Narrative (13:54–17:27)
Discourse: Order in Jesus's *Ekklesia* (chap. 18)
"... *when Jesus completed these sayings*... " (19:1)

VI. Section 5 (chap. 19–25)
Narrative (chap. 19–22)
Discourse: The End and Discipleship (chap. 23–25)
"... *when Jesus completed these sayings*... " (26:1)

VII. The Passion/Resurrection Narrative (chap. 26–28)

Returning to the theme of Jesus's *ekklesia* and that of Moses and the Torah, what makes the correspondence significant is the number *five*. That alone implies that there is a connection. It is hinted at, for example, when Jesus makes clear that he hasn't come to abolish the Law and the Prophets (5:17), while at the same time he doesn't

hesitate to refine how they are to be received. After stating
that "not an iota, not a dot, will pass from the law until
all is accomplished" and that "whoever then relaxes one
of the least of these commandments and teaches men so,
shall be called least in the kingdom of heaven; but he
who does them and teaches them shall be called great in
the kingdom of heaven" (5:18–19), he goes on to interpret the Law *correctly* (implying that the Law has been
mishandled hitherto and not taught according to its true
spirit). In 5:21–48, he is bold to make six "corrections"
to prevailing interpretations, each one beginning with
"You have heard it said... but I say to you..." (verses 21,
27, 31, 33, 38, 43). In short, *he is presenting himself as the Lord
who teaches the true meaning of Torah*, with an authority that
amazes his hearers (7:28–29). Verses 5:43–48 are especially
noteworthy, ending as they do with the words, "You,
therefore, must be perfect, as your heavenly Father is
perfect." In context, this means emulation of the Father's
perfection in demonstrating detached, indiscriminate love
("for he makes his sun rise on the evil and on the good,
and sends rain on the just and on the unjust"). Jesus
is presenting his *halakhah* (in Hebrew, the word simply
means "way," and refers to the proper understanding of
the laws of Torah). And, when Jesus presents the "keys"
to Peter in 16:18–19, he is making him the "chief rabbi"
whose teaching will be the continuation of Jesus's own.

In short, Jesus is not only the interpreter of Moses, but
the One who also possesses the authority to clarify and
even correct the Law itself—in some instances, to make
the commandments stronger by striking at the roots of
transgression in the human heart. So, for example, not
only are murder and adultery forbidden, but also hatred
and unruly sexual desire. Jesus is *the* Lawgiver, superior
to Moses. Likewise, he is the embodiment of mercy and
compassion. He holds these things—Law and mercy—
together. With Jesus (and also with Paul), there is no
opposition between "Law" and "gospel." The similarities

between Jesus and Moses appear as early as Chapter 2, when, as an infant who must flee a child-murdering ruler, he is taken to Egypt by his parents. Later, before he delivers his first discourse, he passes through the waters (in baptism), he "wanders" in the wilderness to be tested for forty days, and delivers his teaching from a mountain. When he meets his disciples in Galilee after the Resurrection, it is also upon a mountain that he gives his final instructions to the gathered disciples. Unlike Mark, who has "Elijah, *with* Moses" appear (Elijah being named first puts priority on his presence), Matthew changes the sequence and names *Moses* first. Jesus is the Lord of the Torah, the gatherer of an *ekklesia* drawn from all nations, and the one who teaches *the* "way."

2.

Not only is Jesus portrayed in the Gospel of Matthew as superior to Moses, but as superior to other biblical figures as well: to Elijah (who appears at the Transfiguration: 17:4–8), to Jonah and Solomon (12:38–45), and to King David, his forebear. Jesus is not only called "the son of David" (1:1) and born in "the city of David" (2:4–5); he is proclaimed in 3:15–17, as were the kings of old, to be "God's son," "the Anointed One" — the kingly Messiah or Christ (compare 2 Sam. 7:14; Ps. 2:7; 89:27). Jesus also resembles David during the time of the latter's misfortunes: like David, he ascends the Mount of Olives, and is betrayed by a boon companion (Matt. 26:30, 47–49; compare 2 Sam. 15:30–31; David's Judas-like betrayer was Ahithophel, originally his trusted adviser).

But Matthew doesn't merely suggest a parallel between Jesus and David, he also *contrasts* them. Jesus is shown to be his forebear's moral superior, bringing blessing where David had pronounced a curse. Before David conquered the Jebusites and entered Jerusalem triumphantly, his enemies had insulted him and his army by proclaiming that even "the blind and the lame" could ward off their attack. The consequence of that jibe, we are told, was that after David took the city, the blind and the lame — "hated by David's soul" — were effectively put under a curse and forbidden entrance to "the house," meaning thereby "the House of the Lord," the Temple (2 Sam. 5:6–8). *In direct contrast*, when Jesus enters Jerusalem, after first being hailed as "the son of David" (Matt. 21:9), Matthew's Gospel tells us in pointed terms that *"the blind and the lame* came to [Jesus] *in the Temple,* and *he healed them"* (21:14; emphasis added). David's "hatred" of the blind and lame is reversed by his "greater Son," who heals them in the very precincts once forbidden to them.

In Matthew's Gospel, Jesus — superior to the kings and prophets who came before him — is the spokesman of God's Wisdom. In Sirach 24, the figure of personified "Wisdom" identifies herself as "the book of the covenant of the Most High God, the law which Moses commanded" (Sir. 24:23). She is embodied in the Torah. Wisdom/Torah thus speaks these words to any who will heed: "Come to me, you who desire me, and eat your fill of my produce. For the remembrance of me is sweeter than honey, and my inheritance sweeter than the honeycomb. Those who eat me will hunger for more, and those who drink me will thirst for more" (Sir. 24:19–21). If those words sound familiar, it is because Jesus says something similar, though using a different analogy, in a passage that is found only in Matthew: "Come to me, all who labor and are heavy laden, and I will give you rest. Take my yoke upon you, and learn from me; for I am gentle and lowly in heart, and you will find rest for your souls. For my yoke is easy, and my burden is light" (Matt. 11:28–30). The early Christians who read this Gospel thus understood that — mystically speaking — Jesus was the definitive conduit of revelation. His teaching was the culmination of the scriptures. Most importantly, his actions were signs of God's mercy, gentleness, wisdom, and healing — thus reflecting the Father's disinterested compassion (Matt. 5:43–48).

Matthew's Gospel highlights, in a way that Mark's does not, the contents of the teachings of Jesus. Luke does the same, but as we will see, there are differences between that Gospel and Matthew's. With Matthew, Jesus's teachings are given primarily to his disciples (for example: "Seeing the crowds, he went up on the mountain, and when he sat down [the position of the teacher] his disciples came to him. And he opened his mouth and taught them"; 5:1-2; "Then the disciples came and said to him, 'Why do you speak to them in parables?' And he answered them, 'To you [the disciples] it has been given to know the secrets of the kingdom of heaven, but to them [those who do not follow him] it has not been given'"; 13:9-10). The five discourses of Jesus in Matthew, which we discussed briefly above, all have to do with the rudimentary teachings necessary to acquire the "kingdom of the heavens" (Matthew says "heavens" where Mark and the others have "God"—likely due to the Judaic reluctance to speak of God directly), and these instructions are meant to establish the terms, principles, aims, and conditions of the *ekklesia* Jesus is "building" (16:18; the word *ekklesia* means "assembly"—the word "synagogue," is a synonym). "Wisdom has built her house..." (Prov. 9:1); Jesus is building a household, which consists of those "who hear these sayings of mine and enact them" (7:24). It shouldn't surprise us, then, that the crux of this Gospel, at the center of its chiasmus, is the third of Jesus's five discourses. It is this discourse (13:1-53) in which he delivers his first series of long, story-like parables, those that are more than pithy one-line analogies.

The first of these parables, that of the sower sowing the seed, is first not only in terms of its coming before the others, but also in terms of its being the basis of all the parables that follow it. The "punchline" is verse 9: "He who has ears, let him hear"; in other words, this is a parable about *listening*. The "soils" in the story—the hardpacked and unreceptive soil of the path, the "rocky ground, where they had not much soil," the thorny patches, and the "good soil" (good because receptive) — indicate the kinds of "hearing" that each of Jesus's hearers might have. What Jesus wants is not those who merely hear, but those who *listen attentively* and consequently develop a desire to hear more; hence his challenging words: "For to him who has will more be given, and he will have abundance; but from him who has not, even what he has will be taken away" (13:12). The meaning is clear: listening to (and enacting) his teaching leads to a deeper understanding of his message, and more "shall be given" to the attentive; but the person who doesn't receive or continue to listen will eventually lose even the little he has understood. The memory of his teachings will dissipate if it isn't constantly kept alive in one's mind.

The parable that follows — that of the wheat and the weeds, or tares, the latter sown in the same field by "an enemy" — is the first in the series to indicate that "at the consummation of the age" those who have heard and are physically in the "kingdom" will be judged — a concept that unsettles the modern mind but would have been entirely expected by the vast majority of peoples in history. There is an unmistakable overlap, it should be evident, of "the kingdom" Christ preaches and the *ekklesia* he is "building." Especially important in Jesus's Matthean parables is that — as 1 Peter 4:17 puts it succinctly — judgment begins "with the household of God."

When Jesus explains the parable of the wheat and weeds to his disciples, it's important to observe that he doesn't explain it in the presence of outsiders. Matthew says pointedly, "Then he left the crowds and went into the house" (13:36), where he explains to them in private its meaning. This physical move — from the outside and open to the inside and closed — is also to be understood as a *spiritual* move. He is, in short, adding "more" to the attentive listeners who already "have" (13:12). Matthew's readers would have understood by this that they, too, are "inside the house" and—more to the point—that they are responsible for what Jesus is teaching them there.

Among the other parables situated at the center of this book, we have one other that, like the parable of the wheat and weeds, stresses both the inclusivity of the kingdom and the judgment that must come to those who have been brought into it. It is the last of the parables in this important section: that of the "net which was thrown into the sea and gathered fish of every kind" (as my brother's translation of the New Testament rightly translates, the "net" is a "large dragnet"). "At the close of the age," "the good" catch will be collected, and "the bad" will be discarded (13:47–50). Once again, modern sensibilities recoil from such a stark declaration. But Jesus's teachings are not concerned with sensibilities, modern or otherwise, but rather that his followers take seriously the responsibilities integral to the kingdom he announces. He had indicated in the parable of the wheat and weeds (unique to Matthew, incidentally, as is the parable of the net and the parable we will look at next) that within the kingdom *both good and evil will coexist in this age.* Those of us who find ourselves appalled in our own time by church scandals, present and past, might appreciate that Jesus seemed fully aware of the mixed moral nature of the assembly he was gathering together. He understood quite well the very worst of human tendencies and, in fact, endured them in his own person (see John 2:24–25). This is why he taught, Matthew suggests, that it is *the disciples* called out of all the nations (ἔθνη, "*ethne*") who will be judged before all others.

Moving, then, from the thirteenth chapter to the final parable of Jesus in Matthew—the culmination of the parables that began with the sower and the seed—we see precisely what sort of kingdom, what sort of *ekklesia*, what sort of standard Jesus establishes among his disciples.

The final discourse of Jesus stretches from the twenty-third chapter through the twenty-fifth. It begins with an excoriation of the religious leaders in Jerusalem and a

stern warning that his disciples are not to emulate their
example (chap. 23). It continues in the next chapter with
eschatological matters, none of which — except those
alluding to the destruction of Jerusalem — are precise
(and, in some of the ancient manuscripts of Matthew, as
in Mark's Gospel, Jesus states: "But about that day and
hour [of the age's consummation] no one knows — neither
the angels of the heavens *nor the Son* — except the Father
only," 24:36, emphasis added; my brother David's translation — quite rightly — includes those words). Chapter
25 then provides three cautionary parables about the
necessity to prepare oneself spiritually. It is the ultimate
parable with which I'm concerned here, in 25:31–46.

Before we look at it, though, we need first to glance at
the last words of Jesus in the Gospel. Unlike Luke, but like
John, there is no description of Jesus ascending into the
heavens. Instead, we have his promise *to remain* among his
disciples (in spirit): "I am with you always, to the close
of the age" (28:20). Before that, he says to the eleven
disciples on a mountain in Galilee: "Go therefore and
make disciples of all nations [ἔθνη] ... teaching them to
observe all that I have commanded you ..." (28:19–20).
What is envisioned here is that the teachings of Jesus
will be spread beyond the bounds of the Hebrew people
and sown among the "nations," the "gentiles," the *ethne*.

Looking back, then, to Jesus's final parable — arguably,
the most important in Matthew — that of the judgment
at the end of the age, we must see in it not a judgment of
"the world," *but of those who have received the scattered seed
of Jesus's teachings and responded in their various ways*. Here,
of course, we recall the different "soils," the mingling
of wheat and tares, the good and bad fish — all regarded
as those who have heard and either listened attentively,
enacting what they heard ... or not. It is "all the nations
[ἔθνη]" who are gathered, and what is meant is those who
have been "made disciples [out] of all nations." This is
why the standard used to *separate* them is the standard

Jesus has presented all along throughout the Gospel, from the Sermon on the Mount onwards: "I was hungry and you gave me [or didn't] something to eat, I was thirsty and you gave me [or didn't] a drink, I was a stranger and you gave me [or didn't] hospitality, naked and you clothed me [or did not], I was ill and you looked after me [or did not], I was in prison and you came to me [or did not]" (25:34–35; 42–43; DBHNT[4]). These words may even indicate one way that Jesus remains "with them always, to the close of the age" — "*I* was there before your eyes as one hungry, thirsty, a stranger, naked, ill, imprisoned...What did you do in response to my presence *in those in need whom you encountered*?"

The sort of kingdom, the sort of *ekklesia* or *church* that Jesus intends is one that lives up to his unequivocal standards. It is meant to reflect the Father's perfection in love, offering a foretaste of what lies beyond the consummation of this age. In this present age, Jesus is saying in Matthew's Gospel, the church is still being built, the kingdom is still growing from the seed of his sowing. When we pray to the Father in our secret inner "room" (Matt. 6:6), it is there that the teachings he sowed take root and spring up within us. When we "build our houses" as disciples, they are to be built on rock, not sand (7:24–27). And building on the rock means, quite explicitly, to listen attentively to "these sayings of mine and enacting them" (7:24). What is to be enacted is the mercy, compassion, and love that Jesus requires of us. And, in those justly famous words of St John of the Cross, "in the evening of life, we will be judged on love alone."

3.

When we look closely at any of the Gospels, we have little choice but to ask questions about what German biblical scholars referred to as the *Sitz im Leben* — the "life

---

[4] D. B. Hart, *The New Testament: A Translation*, 2nd edition (New Haven, 2023).

situation" or "life setting" — of the communities which produced and read them. At best, we can only conjecture about those settings based on the scant evidence we have. Recently, within academic circles focusing on New Testament studies, this approach has been called into question; perhaps, it has been argued, the Gospels and Acts are works of independent literary creation, not reflective of any community other than that of Graeco-Roman *literati*. In other words, it's not a given that any specific Christian community was responsible for the writing of these books. Nonetheless, there is much more evidence, internal and external, to the contrary: that each of the Gospels reflects its own provenance. In an era such as the first century, when even slaves were trained to read and write as their masters had need, it's hardly inconceivable that there would be competent, culturally aware writers within the Christian communities. We also know from the Epistles in the New Testament (and other early Christian literature) that these churches included persons who were well-to-do and, we can be sure, those who were schooled and conversant with the literature of the day. In short, then, we should take seriously what suggests itself as the probable "life situation" of Matthew. Conceivably, such an approach may help to answer a rather mystifying question: *Why does the writer double so many characters and even, in one case, donkeys, where Mark and Luke mention just one person and one donkey?*

I presented the problem a few pages back with these observations: In Matthew, there are *two* demoniacs, instead of just one as in Mark and Luke; two *pairs* of blind men, unlike the other two Synoptics; and Jesus rides into Jerusalem on an ass *and* a foal — *two* animals — rather than on the single animal specified by both Mark and Luke. I mentioned above that this tendency to double, in my view, is associated with a significant theme that Matthew considers important. Important for whom? Doubtless, for *his church*. To get at what I mean, we should look at something I also brought up earlier: The *strained relations* between the Matthean *ekklesia* and *other Jewish communities*. Part of that strain, I suggested, may have been the result of the reception of uncircumcised gentiles as members of the Christian church, probably in Antioch and its vicinity.

Even a cursory reading of Matthew indicates that the author was concerned with two features of the Antiochian church's identity.

First, it was primarily a *Jewish* community with a mission to make gentile converts, a fact made clear especially in Matthew 28:19–20. The gentiles most likely to have become members of Matthew's church would have been those who had previously been "God-fearers" — those who believed in the God of Israel and attended the synagogue, but who stopped short of receiving circumcision, which in turn would have meant adopting fully the observance of the whole Mosaic Law (what, in fact, we see the Pharisees insisting on in the Gospels). Such complete conversion would have put a social wedge between gentiles and their non-Jewish families, institutions, and friends. We should bear in mind that the issue in the earliest era of the *ekklesia* or "church" — a term that suggests to us an institution *separate* from Judaism, but that certainly had no such connotation in that period — was *not:* "How do Jews become Christians?" Such a formulation would have made no sense in their context. The question for them — and the one that underlies the Jerusalem council in Acts 15 and Paul's contention with Peter in Galatians 2 (both these texts being focused on the "life situation" of the *ekklesia* in Antioch in Syria) — was: *"How should gentiles be included as members of the Jewish faith* (a term that is something of an excusable anachronism) *through Jesus the Messiah?"*

According to Acts 15, the mother *ekklesia* in Jerusalem, headed by James, the Lord's brother, had stipulated that inclusion of gentile converts required the latter "abstain from what has been sacrificed to idols and from

blood and from what is strangled and from unchastity"
(Acts 15:29). Circumcision for male converts and the
obligation to observe the Law in its entirety was waived
for them. The book of Acts was written years after Paul
had penned his anxious and angry Letter to the Galatians, and its account of the resolution of the problem
in Antioch had acquired a rosier hue than Paul's letter
indicates, written not many years after the actual events.
Paul tells us that Peter had been associating freely with the
gentile converts, probably even sharing table fellowship
with them (something Jews and gentiles didn't normally
do), until "certain men came from James," the leader
of the Jewish-Christian mother church in Jerusalem,
and "fearing the circumcision party" (meaning those
same Jewish believers from Jerusalem, many of whom
no doubt insisted on circumcision for gentile converts),
Peter had withdrawn himself from mingling with the
gentile believers. Consequently, others — including Paul's
fellow-missionary, Barnabas — had followed Peter's bad
example, effectively breaking fellowship (Gal. 2:11 ff.).
With these few verses in Paul's letter, we have a glimpse
of the two ends of the Petrine-Pauline tradition of the
first century perilously pulling in opposite directions:
one direction (the "Petrine," or actually the "Jamesian") being its Judaic, Torah-observant identity, and Paul
pulling in the other direction, that of full participation
(not requiring circumcision) and table fellowship for
(formerly) gentile followers of Jesus.

If modern scholars are correct (not that I'd stake anything on it), there is close to a thirty-year gap between
Paul's Epistles (written in the 50s) and Matthew's Gospel
(probably written in the 80s). Matthew, as we have noted,
most likely had Antioch for its provenance, and even
after three decades the matter of Judean-gentile relations
remains front and center. What Matthew's emphases suggest is that there existed in his community what might be
called a modified "Petrine/ Jamesian" position, holding

the Mosaic Law and tradition in high regard — "Whoever then relaxes one of the least of these commandments and teaches men so, shall be called least in the kingdom of heaven; but he who does them and teaches them shall be called great in the kingdom of heaven" (5:19) — which is starkly unlike the tendency of Paul to present the Law as essentially good but, through the mishandling of intermediaries, flawed and burdensome and unable to save (see, for example, Gal. 3:19–25; 2 Cor. 3:7–11; Rom. 7:1–6). But even a modified Petrine/Jamesian position such as Matthew's evidently ran contrary to what was considered acceptable by other Judaic communities. No doubt, the conviction that Jesus was Messiah and Lord created tensions with these other communities, but the inclusion of gentiles as full members of the rival "synagogue" of Jesus would have been viewed as beyond the pale, permitting gentile uncleanness to take root in its very midst.

So, the *second* aspect implicit to Matthew's Gospel has to do with the church's relations with other Jewish groups, and it seems that they may have been tense indeed. Most scholars assume that we can read into Matthew's elaboration of Jesus's polemics against the Pharisees a reflection of the situation at the time the Gospel was written. Comparing the lengthy denunciation Jesus issues in Matthew 23 with Mark's much more modest version (Mark 12:38–40) suggests as much. It comes across as "padded." Opposition to Jesus's message by the Judean religious authorities is a recurring, salient theme throughout Matthew (9:10–13; 12:1–8, 24–28; 15:1–9; 16:1–4; 19:3–9; 22:15–20, 34–40). It would be anachronistic to regard his emphasis on this conflict as an attack on "the Jews" by "Christians," but instead as two Jewish factions at odds with one another about a significant issue; and, as the note in *The Jewish Annotated New Testament* so succinctly states, "Adherents of a particular group [in this case, both sides were Jewish] or set of beliefs often polemicize most strongly against those who share similar, but not identical, beliefs."[5] That one of the bones of contention was the issue of how gentiles were to be received—with or without circumcision and all that circumcision entailed— seems plausible, given how much Matthew stresses the mission to the "nations" (ἔθνη, "ethne" = "gentiles"). The message of Jesus is, in Matthew, intended for all peoples. In this, Matthew agrees with Paul, even if the two differ in how they view the place and status of the Law.

Early in Matthew's Gospel, in fact, gentiles receive the revelation of Christ in the persons of the Magi (2:1–12). Some chapters later, Jesus (shockingly, in that context) heals the slave of a Roman centurion, even declaring, "Truly, I say to you, not even in Israel have I found such faith" as that displayed by the gentile soldier (8:5–13). Later still, a Canaanite woman approaches Jesus to obtain healing for her daughter, and Jesus—quite obviously testing her faith—rebuffs her. When she openly shows her faith with a quick-witted rejoinder, Jesus praises her: "O woman, great is your faith!" (15:21–28).[6] In all three of these accounts, we have gentiles showing faith in the God of Israel, and on this basis, they are received by Jesus, even when he tests one of them rudely to demonstrate to his Jewish disciples the genuineness of this gentile woman's devotion. So, as we noted above, when the ἔθνη ("nations," "gentiles," "peoples") are gathered for judgment (25:31– 46), these are the same ἔθνη that the disciples are sent into the world to baptize and teach Christ's commandments (28:19–20). Matthew's Gospel, then, stresses both the observant Jewishness of his community *and* its dominical mission to gather disciples from all peoples. *Both* Jew and gentile are "ransomed, healed, restored, forgiven."

---

[5] Amy-Jill Levine and Marc Zvi Brettler, eds., *The Jewish Annotated New Testament* (New York, 2011), 41.

[6] It's interesting to compare the parallel version of Mark 7:24– 30. Matthew's account intensifies Jesus's initial—feigned, in my opinion—rejection of her. Uncharacteristically, Mark gives us the milder version.

Here we have the clue to unraveling the mystery of why it is Matthew *doubles* human characters—two demoniacs, two pairs of blind men—and that pair of donkeys. There is no way to know for sure, but I tend to believe that Matthew is saying through his symbolic doublings that *both* Jews and gentiles, through Jesus Christ, are included in God's one people and kingdom. No one is to be excluded; all the nations are to be blessed in the Seed of Abraham. The Father is God of all: "His kingdom ruleth over all," as the Psalm puts it (103:19).

This message, of course, met with opposition from those who, on the one hand, saw it as compromising the Torah, threatening to undermine the source of cohesion—adherence to the entirety of the Law—within the Jewish community. On the other hand, the Pauline pull was even more extreme in its view of the Law, more critical of its value in the life of the followers of Jesus. Matthew (like the Epistle of James) stands somewhere in the middle—unwilling to regard the Law as obsolete ("Whoever then relaxes one of the least of these commandments and teaches men so, shall be called least in the kingdom of heaven; but he who does them and teaches them shall be called great in the kingdom of heaven"; 5:18), but equally unwilling to demand that gentiles enter the kingdom of heaven on any other basis than their faithfulness and willingness to become disciples of Christ.

Meanwhile, all those pairs of demoniacs and blind men and donkeys that Matthew presents us with are reminders—signs—that Jesus's message ("Repent [transform your thoughts], for the kingdom of heaven is at hand"; 4:17) is an invitation to all the world. The only possibility of exclusion lies in the ultimate judgment of each person's life—and that judgment, we are told, will be based on our treatment of others as their needs present themselves to us. It's a tough message, but a gracious one; open to all, but one that takes our lives, convictions, and actions with utmost seriousness.

IV

The Gospel of Luke

1.

Among the Gospels, that ascribed to Luke is the most literary. Also, unlike the other three Gospels, it isn't a stand-alone book, but rather the first half of a two-part work that might be called "Luke-Acts." The New Testament canon inserts John's Gospel between the first half and its "other half," the book of Acts. Both works stand out in that they are clearly the composition of an erudite man, conversant with the narrative style of his age, and exhibiting a thoroughgoing acquaintance with the Septuagint (LXX)—the Greek version of the Hebrew Bible that was commonly used in Hellenistic synagogues. The tradition maintains that the author was Luke, "the beloved physician," a close companion of Paul (Col. 4:14; Philem. 24; 2 Tim. 4:11). Irenaeus, Tertullian, Clement of Alexandria, and the "Muratorian Canon" all credit the Gospel and Acts to him. From the time of Irenaeus (late second century), it has been claimed that its place of origin was Achaea in southern Greece, where the city of Corinth was dominant. A number of modern scholars have challenged the claim that Luke was the author, and that Achaea was its provenance. That noted, there's nonetheless very little reason to dismiss out of hand the traditional view. This is certainly a plausible attribution, if indeed Luke had been a Greek convert and physician (quite often, physicians were slaves in the Graeco-Roman world, although Luke had evidently gained his freedom), and an educated man with literary abilities. Whether he was or wasn't the author, though, Luke-Acts seems most likely to have been written in the 80s. Our chief concern, though, isn't with the theories and occasional wrangling of New Testament scholars (a sensitive and sometimes argumentative lot, as it happens, especially when it comes to questions that are beyond any hope of resolution this side of the Parousia). Rather, my focus is on a few aspects of the text that indicate the overall *meaning* the work had — and still has — for its believing readers.

Perhaps the first question to pose is this: Who was Theophilus, the person to whom the author addresses both parts of his diptych (Luke 1:1–4; Acts 1:1)? The uninspiring answer is that we don't know. The name is Greek and means "friend of God." Was Theophilus an official of some sort, knowledgeable about Christianity but not necessarily a believer? Probably not, since Luke says that his work is to confirm to him the "narrative of the things which have been accomplished among us," so that Theophilus "may know the truth concerning the things of which [he has] been informed." Those "things of which [Theophilus had] been informed" had perhaps been contained in other "orderly narratives" about Jesus and his apostles — other Gospels (Mark and Matthew possibly among them) and other books of the apostles' "acts." In other words, Luke possibly intended to improve on earlier written works. His was a generation that had heard the testimony of the "eyewitnesses" and, having accepted that the expected end of the age was not immediately on the horizon (else, why write down any "orderly narratives" at all?), was now committed to chronicling the history of Jesus and the earliest recollections of the church's beginnings and spread, with a view to the future. Luke was writing theological history (God's fulfillment of his promises to Abraham and his descendants in Christ is a central theme) and his work is consciously literary in nature. What I mean by that is that he labored to produce literature of good and lasting quality that could stand side by side with other literature of equal quality. It's not a work by or for a semi-literate community, but one that has capable scribes within its circle. Which brings me back to Theophilus. He was, it seems, a disciple, one who had been thoroughly instructed already. And, quite possibly, "he" may not even have been a single identifiable person at all. "Friend of God" could be a name that refers generically to any "disciple" or "follower" of Jesus. Again, we don't know; but we do know that the style of Luke-Acts is similar to those well-honed narratives in classical literature that recounted the lives and adventures of various model personages.

In the chapters on Mark and Matthew, we stressed the importance of taking note of each book's chiasmus. But in the Gospel of Luke's case, what we have is the first half of a longer work. The overall work's second half—which parallels the Gospel in many of its features[1]—is the book of Acts. What this means is that we must look to the single event that is *described at the conclusion of the Gospel* and then *repeated with additional details in the first chapter of Acts* to find an interpretive "center" for both books. That significant center is the event of the Ascension of Christ. Everything in the Gospel leads up to that moment, and everything that occurs in Acts flows out of it. *The essential motif of the Ascension is kingly enthronement*: Jesus is the Lord, the true and eternal Emperor. Given that Luke emphasizes the significance of Jesus in world history, the Ascension as the centerpiece is perfectly congruent.

The trajectory begins nearly at the outset of the Gospel. To Mary at the Annunciation, the angel Gabriel[2] says:

---

[1] Healing of paralysis (Luke 5:17–26; Acts 3:1–11; 9:32–35); raising the dead (Luke 7:11–17; 8:40–56; Acts 9:36–43; 20:7–12); casting out demons (Luke 4:31–37; Acts 5:16; 8:7; 19:11–16); healing of fever (Luke 4:3–39; Acts 28:8); parallels between Jesus and Paul (Luke 23:18 = Acts 21:36, 22:22; Luke 18:32, 24:6–7 = Acts 21:11, 28:17; Luke 23:4, 13–15, 22, 41, 47 = Acts 22:25, 23:1, 9, 29; 24:12–13, 16, 19–20; 25:8, 10–11, 18, 25–26; 26:21–23, 31–32; 28:17–19); Jesus's prophecies in the Gospel fulfilled in the life of his followers (Luke 9:22 = Acts 3:21; Lk. 21:12–15 = Acts 4:3–5; 14; Luke 9:5 = Acts 13:51).

[2] Gabriel (whose rather strange name—גַּבְרִיאֵל—means "God,

"He will be great, and will be called the Son of the Most High; and the Lord God will give to him the throne of his father David, and he will reign over the house of Jacob for ever; and of his kingdom there will be no end" (Luke 1:32–33). This echoes God's words to David in 2 Samuel 7:13, 17, which are picked up in Psalm 89:29, 36: "I will establish [David's] line forever, and his throne as the days of the heavens... His line shall endure forever, his throne as long as the sun before me..." The Ascension, inferring as it does a *heavenly* enthronement, assures the reader that Jesus, the "Son of David," *has indeed established David's line everlastingly*. At his baptism (notably, in Luke—unlike in Mark and Matthew—Jesus's baptism is referred to only in passing), the voice of the Father declares: "Thou art my beloved Son; with thee I am well pleased" (3:23; see 9:35)—words that pick up on the language of the second Psalm, an "enthronement" psalm: "You are my son, today I have begotten you..." (Ps. 2:7). Likewise, Mary is raised to queenly status in the greeting she receives from Elizabeth (1:43). As I wrote in *Silent Rosary*: "To see this, we need only consider what the phrase 'Mother of the Lord' [which is how Elizabeth addresses Mary] implies in this context. The term referred to the 'queen mother' in the times of Judah's and Israel's kings, and this is undoubtedly the intended association here. The mother of the king held high status in the kingdom."[3] Here and throughout the Gospel, then, the movement is steadily in the direction of Jerusalem (the seat of the House of David), where Jesus will not only

---

my man") appears, significantly, as a messenger who interprets visions of the future in Daniel 8 and 9, and he reappears in the pseudepigraphical book of 1 Enoch (chapters 9, 10, 20, and 40).

[3] Addison Hodges Hart, *Silent Rosary: A Contemplative, Exegetical, and Iconographic Tour Through the Mysteries* (Eugene, 2021), 40–41. In the accompanying footnote, I added: "The mothers of the kings in Jerusalem are listed with the names of their sons in the books of the Kings: 1 Kings 14:21; 15:2, 10; 2 Kings 12:1; 14:2; 15:2, 33; 18:2; 21:1, 19; 22:1; 23:31, 36. Cf., too, 1 Kings 15:13."

die and rise from the sepulcher but ascend from there to his state of eternal cosmic lordship.

And his lordship is indeed both cosmic in scope and inclusive of the whole of humanity, both Jews and gentiles. He is, as presented in Luke, the heart of human history. Luke's version of Jesus's genealogy, then, doesn't begin as Matthew's does with Abraham. Rather, Luke goes further back, to the beginning, tracing Jesus's ancestry all the way to "Adam, the son of God" (3:23–38). The *meaning* of Luke's genealogy of Jesus is more important than questions about its historicity: he is telling us that Jesus's humanity is related essentially to *all* races and peoples and, therefore, the salvation he brings is inclusive of *all* mankind. In Paul's language, Jesus is perfectly "the second [and last] Adam."

To underscore Jesus's importance in history, Luke pointedly provides historical context—for example, when he comes to be baptized by his cousin, John: "In the fifteenth year of the reign of Tiberius Caesar, Pontius Pilate being governor of Judea, and Herod being tetrarch of Galilee, and his brother Philip tetrarch of the region of Ituraea and Trachonitis, and Lysanias tetrarch of Abilene, in the high-priesthood of Annas and Caiaphas..." (3:1–2). These background details apply the cement of verifiable facts to the narrative. He grounds the story of Jesus in the chronicles of history.

So, it shouldn't surprise us that there is an emphasis in this Gospel and also in Acts on the inclusion of the gentiles into the people of God, particularly as a fulfillment of God's promise to Abraham and his descendants. It is *explicitly* a focus in Luke-Acts, and especially notable in the second book (for example, with Peter's vision and the conversion of Cornelius and his family in Acts 10; see also Acts 15:6–11). Significantly, too, it is *implicit* in the appointing by Jesus of *seventy* additional disciples (or seventy-two in some manuscripts)—recounted only in Luke (Luke 10:1 ff.). Based on Genesis 10, the Hebrew tradition spoke of *seventy* nations of the gentiles. The *twelve* apostles correspond to the *twelve* tribes of Israel; as Jesus says to them at the last supper: "I assign to you, as my Father assigned to me, a kingdom, that you may eat and drink at my table in my kingdom, and sit on thrones *judging the twelve tribes of Israel*" (22:29–30; emphasis added). The additional seventy whom Jesus commissions foreshadow the mission to the "seventy nations" of the gentiles.

In Luke, Jesus goes to the cross with dignity and self-composure—in other words, *as a king.* In 22:43–44, verses unfortunately omitted in some manuscripts and consequently in some modern translations, Jesus's prayer on the Mount of Olives is depicted heroically as an ἀγωνία ("*agonia*")—a "struggle" or "contest": "And there appeared to him an angel from heaven, strengthening him. And being in an agony [ἀγωνίᾳ] he prayed more earnestly; and his sweat became like great drops of blood falling down upon the ground." There is no mention in Luke of the crown of thorns—and its absence was probably not an oversight on the part of the author. Jesus declares to the religious authorities gathered to judge him: "But from now on the Son of man shall be seated at the right hand of the power of God" (22:69). He stands before Pilate and Herod, not deigning to address them, except for a single enigmatic remark to the former (23:1 ff.). He solemnly prophesies to the women in the Jerusalem crowd as he is led to his crucifixion (23:28–31). He pardons his executioners (23:34). He promises the repentant criminal crucified beside him, who pleads that he be remembered by Jesus "when you come into your Kingdom," that "today you will be with me in Paradise" (23:42–43). And where Mark and Matthew have Jesus crying out the stark words of Psalm 22 (21):1—"My God, my God, why hast thou forsaken me?"—Luke instead has Jesus echoing the words of Psalm 31:5: "Father, into thy hands I commit my spirit!" (23:46). Even on the cross, Jesus displays his

kingly nobility and authority. Luke's theology of the cross
is simultaneously a theology of Christ's regal glory—a
glory tested, martyred, put to death, yes, but ultimately
triumphant. Again, the centerpiece in Luke-Acts is the
Ascension and the reign of Jesus Christ over the nations
and the entire course of human history.

One last and not inconsequential thing to note in
this section is that Luke's Gospel has given the church
some of its most staple prayers and canticles, said and
sung daily in liturgy and private devotion by countless
Christians in every language, for two millennia. Without
Luke, we would have neither the Jesus Prayer (18:13) nor
the "Hail, Mary" (1:28, 42); nor would we have the *Magnificat* (1:46–55), the *Benedictus* (1:68–79), and the *Nunc
Dimittis* (2:29–32). Not only was the author of Luke-Acts
a proficient writer of prose, but also our premier recorder
of the church's earliest—and, subsequently, ceaselessly
used—Christian hymnody.

2.

Unlike the other Gospels, as we noted above, the
interpretive key comes at the book's end, since its chiastic structure embraces two volumes. Everything in the
Gospel, as we said, leads up to the Ascension, emblematic
of Christ's cosmic lordship, and everything in Acts flows
from the power of the Spirit that the ascended Christ
bestows on his apostles. Hence, the book of Acts ends
on a note of accomplishment: with Paul, the message of
Christ has reached Rome, the heart of the world, and
from there it will extend to earth's ends. It doesn't conclude with the martyrdom of Paul, as one could have
expected, even though Acts was most likely written years
after his death. Luke's message is centered on Christ's
resurrection and the consequent growth of the kingdom,
which is reflected in the final words of the book of Acts:
"And [Paul] lived [in Rome] two whole years at his own
expense, and welcomed all who came to him, *preaching*

the kingdom of God and teaching about the Lord Jesus Christ quite openly and unhindered" (Acts 28:30–31; emphasis added). The heavenly reign of Christ and his gift of the Spirit, which empowers the apostles' mission, ensure that God's promise that the House of David would reign everlastingly is accomplished.

One has only to read the inaugural proclamation of Peter, announced to representatives of the nations on the day of Pentecost, to see clearly what lies at the heart of Luke's good news (Acts 2:14–36). Since Luke presents his message as the "glad tidings" of the Messiah's eternal sovereignty, he puts great emphasis on the "prevenient" grace and mercy that are the hallmark of this sovereignty ("Glory to God in the highest, and on earth peace among men with whom he is pleased!"; Luke 2:14). God's favor comes first, and — once perceived by those who have ears to hear — human beings have only to respond in faithfulness to it.

This aspect of the proclamation of the kingdom is demonstrated again and again in the Gospel. The *grace* of God ("gift" from the Greek χάρις, *"charis"*) is revealed in Luke by Jesus's magnanimity demonstrated toward others *without them requesting it beforehand.* It isn't misreading the text to say that these are instances of *kingly* largesse.

There are numerous examples one could cite. When one begins to see this feature of the Gospel, it becomes evident almost everywhere in the text. But a few illustrations will suffice. Jesus raises the dead son of a woman in Nain, simply because he sees her weeping and has compassion for her (7:11–17). In the same chapter, he is dining in the home of Simon, a Pharisee, when a woman of immoral reputation enters uninvited, bathes his feet with her tears, and dries them with her hair. Jesus tells those present who are quick to remonstrate that it's because she has been forgiven her sins that she has displayed her love with such extravagance. When and how she experienced this forgiveness, we are never told, but

Jesus confirms that she has indeed been forgiven: "'I tell you, her sins, which were many, have been forgiven; hence she has shown great love...' Then he said to her, 'Your sins are forgiven... Your faith has saved you; go in peace'" (7:47–48, 50; NRSV). Another example: when Jesus enters Jericho, a tax collector named Zacchaeus climbs a tree to get a look at this sensational rabbi. Jesus sees him and invites himself to Zacchaeus's home to lodge. By indicating that he doesn't shun this "sinner's" hospitality, Jesus shows the tax collector a magnanimity that shocks the villagers (19:1–10). One final example: as Jesus is crucified, he prays for his executioners: "Father, forgive them; for they know not what they do" (23:34). In all these instances (and there are others), what is revealed is grace: grace that precedes even the desire for mercy, that goes beyond all expectation, that can only be received (not earned), for which one should show gratitude (see 17:11–19), *and*—and this is important—necessitates a response through the transformation of one's thoughts, words, and deeds.

This last point can be illustrated by taking note specifically of the parables of Jesus that are unique to Luke. Luke has parables in common with Matthew and Mark, but there are no less than *eleven* parables of Jesus that are recorded only in his Gospel (Matthew and Mark, it should be noted, also contain parables found respectively only in each of them). Of these eleven, just one parable—that of the barren fig tree (13:6–9)—finds a rough parallel in the account of Jesus's cursing of the fig tree in Mark and Matthew, but it has an altogether different import than Jesus's action possesses in those Gospels (cf. Mark 11:12 ff.; Matt. 21:18 ff.). The rest of the eleven uniquely Lukan parables are devoid even of that shred of a hint of a parallel; but they all, in one way or another, are about the grace of God in Christ, and what is expected from those who are beneficiaries of it.

The eleven parables are:

(1) *The Parable of the Two Debtors* (Luke 7:41–43), which is told in conjunction with the account of the woman who bathes Jesus's feet with her tears. The meaning of the story is simple: the one who is *forgiven more* (and knows it) will demonstrate *greater love* in return.

(2) *The Parable of the Good Samaritan* (Luke 10:30–37), which is told in response to "a certain lawyer" who "tests" Jesus (vs. 25). The meaning, again easily ascertained, is that everyone is potentially our "neighbor," to whom we should be prepared to give aid when there is need (cf. Matt. 25:31–46). *Mercy received begets mercy bestowed.*

(3) *The Parable of the Importunate Friend* (Luke 11:5–13) is one of three parables in which God is implicitly compared to very unlikely analogs: a friend who *begrudges* having his sleep disturbed (here), an *unscrupulous* Lord (16:1–9), and an *unjust* judge (18:1–8). The point of such unflattering comparisons is, in effect, to ask the question, "*If* such a person as this will do such-and-such in these circumstances, *how much more* can we expect the Father—who is the ultimate good—to do thus-and-so?" Here, the point of the story is that *the disciple should be persistent in prayer*, just as the man wanting three loaves is persistent in disturbing his friend. God will respond graciously. *But note*: Jesus clarifies what it is that his hearers should be persistent in requesting from the Father in prayer: *a holy spirit* or *the Holy Spirit*. This parable is the basis of the idea that the goal of prayer and discipline is *the acquisition of the Spirit*—that is, the cleansing, transfiguring presence of God within oneself. In Christian mystical theology, this concept is equated with the kingdom of God (see 17:20–21).

(4) *The Parable of the Rich Fool* (Luke 12:16–21) is one of the parables that stresses how wealth should be used by followers of Christ. Someone in the crowd listening to Jesus says to him (evidently, not hearing a word that he has said); "Teacher, tell my brother to divide his inheritance with me" (vs. 13). Jesus ignores the request and

tells this story to warn against avarice. And, after he tells the parable, he goes on to teach at length that *God gives freely, and therefore so should all those who seek his kingdom* (vss. 22–34).

(5) *The Parable of the Barren Fig Tree* (Luke 13:6–9) is a parable of warning. God's patience is long, but *he expects "fruit"*—defined as "change of heart" (vs. 5).

(6) *The Parable of the Lost Coin* (Luke 15:8–10) is one of three parables in Chapter 15 that tell of God's grace in restoring what was lost. All three of the stories are told in response to "the Pharisees and the scribes [who] murmured, saying, 'This man receives sinners and eats with them'" (to eat with someone in that culture implied or established solidarity with them, a bond of sorts). The first is the parable of the lost sheep (vss. 3–7; also found in Matt. 18:10–14). The third (see directly below) is that of the prodigal son. The meaning of the parable of the lost "drachma"—a silver coin—has the same meaning as the first of the three: *God searches for the lost, not wanting that any should perish.*

(7) *The Parable of the Prodigal Son* (Luke 15:11–32), like the lost coin parable immediately preceding it, shows—in the person of the father in the story—that *God receives back "sinners" with open arms* (in the parable, the father doesn't even wait for his lost son's declaration of repentance), despite those who regard such graciousness as a dereliction of justice and moral duty. The elder son resents the father's charitableness and complains about it (like the Pharisees and scribes mentioned in verse 2), but the father is adamant that his actions are right, implying that the disgruntled elder son should imitate him.

(8) *The Parable of the Unrighteous Lord* (Luke 16:1–9) is, once again, about the use of wealth. The fact that the unscrupulous lord admires the even more unscrupulous steward is not intended to encourage a lack of honesty, obviously. Like the parable of the importunate friend above, it's an analogy: *If* the unrighteous lord

could admire the generosity shown by the unscrupulous steward, though it was done for the wrong reasons, *how much more* will God bless those "stewards" of his who imitate his own generosity and expend it on those in need — thus making "friends" (in the heavens?) who will intercede on behalf of their benefactor? *Grace begets grace — or it should.*

(9) *The Parable of the Rich Man and Lazarus* (Luke 16:19–31) is likewise about the use of wealth and picks up on the theme of the previous parable. The rich man — who has never noticed the impoverished Lazarus at his own doorstep in life (even though the dogs showed him kindness) — seeks Lazarus's intercession for his equally purblind and stingy brothers after both he and the poor man have died. Abraham answers on behalf of Lazarus with a definite "no." The point Jesus is making is a truly piercing one: *how we have lived (i.e., responded to God's grace) has consequences beyond this age — we will reap what we have sown* (it can be compared with the parable of the last judgment in Matthew 25:31–46).

(10) *The Parable of the Unjust Judge* (Luke 18:1–8) is similar to the parable of the importunate friend above. We are told straightforwardly what it means: "And he told them a parable, to the effect that they ought always to pray and not lose heart." *Persistence in prayer — a life of prayer — is what is here being encouraged.* Once again, *if* the unjust judge acts on behalf of the bothersome widow, *how much more* will "God vindicate his elect, who cry to him day and night?" The concluding statement Jesus appends to the story is very sobering indeed, reminding us that faithfulness is the expected response to grace: "Nevertheless, when the Son of man comes, will he find faith on earth?"

(11) *The Parable of the Pharisee and the Tax Collector* (Luke 18:9–14) follows directly on the previous parable, and once more we are told precisely what the parable is about: "He also told this parable to some who trusted in

themselves that they were righteous and despised others."
The prayer that the tax collector (almost a synonym for
"sinner" in that context) *repeatedly* prays, and for which
he goes home "justified" ("pronounced righteous")
expresses humility and need: "God, be merciful to me
a sinner!" (This repeated invocation would become, of
course, enshrined in the Jesus Prayer.) *He receives grace,
in other words, because he is open to it.* The Pharisee, who
assumes that, surely, he must be in God's good graces,
goes to his house *not* justified. Worse, he seems oblivious
to that terrifying reality.

These, then, are the eleven parables unique to Luke.
Taken together, they tell us that (a) God's grace is offered
to all, even those who are deemed "sinners" (meaning
those who have gone off-course and become lost); (b)
once God's generosity, revealed as mercy and forgiveness,
has been realized by us, we are to exhibit a like generosity
in all our interactions with others; (c) if we are wealthy,
we are to use our wealth for the sake of others, even to
the point of giving it away (this gets a lot of attention
in both the Gospel and Acts); (d) our lives should be
characterized by ongoing prayerfulness and faithfulness;
and (e) we are to be humble, not despising others or
becoming sanctimonious.

Luke's good news, then, is what we need to hear at the
deepest level of our souls, if we are willing to be honest
with ourselves. Whereas there are certain "spiritualities"
that presume we naturally have resources within us to "do
it" all by ourselves, with no outside help—whether that
means self-directed moral improvement or the attain-
ment of some form of "mindful" enlightenment—Luke's
Gospel presents us with unvarnished truth instead: *We
don't. Effectual grace must precede confidence.*

Most of us come to know very well—as we grow in
years and have had time to make serious errors, hurt
others and ourselves, discover how dominated by our
desires and unruly passions we have been and still are,

and maybe much worse — that we are in need of forgiveness, inner cleansing, revivification, and a change of heart. As Luke presents it, the message of Jesus is that forgiveness has been bestowed on all *preveniently*; it was given before we ever thought to ask for it. Before we awakened to our need for it, grace was already a reality. But once realized, we must be prepared to have our hearts and actions changed radically — to "take up [our] cross each day" (9:23) — and live in accord with the largesse that we have been shown. God is patient with us as we cooperate with him in our own cultivation, but every aspect of our lives — including our wealth and our own bodies — is answerable to the ascended Lord. And so, with that understanding, we persevere in prayer (communion with him), seek the acquisition of God's Spirit, and act as we are bidden to do by Christ. All this flows from Christ, ascended and sovereign, and it is the foundational good news of Luke-Acts.

V
The Gospel of John

1.

By this point, readers know that what lies at the literal (or literary) center of each Gospel is also central to its meaning. As we have seen, at the center of Mark was the Transfiguration of Jesus (Mark 9:1 ff.), at the core of Matthew was the first series of Jesus's long parables (Matt. 13:1–53), and in the case of Luke—because it was one half of a two-volume work—the thematic center-point (the Ascension of Jesus) came at the Gospel's conclusion, repeated with varying detail in the first chapter of Acts. What this should tell us is that, while the narratives of Jesus's passion and death are lengthy and vitally important in every Gospel, none of the Gospels should be understood as *centered* on the cross. In other words, Jesus's suffering is something he is destined to *pass through* (and those who follow him are called to live according to the same spiritual pattern and possibly even embrace martyrdom in faithfulness to him), but the real and everlasting destination is *glorification*, the *proclamation of glad tidings*, and the *gathering of disciples*. When we come to John's Gospel, which stands out among the four in many ways, that familiar feature holds true, despite its differences from the others. The interpretive crux of John is 11:38–44: the raising of Lazarus from the dead. John's Gospel, then, is concentrated on "the resurrection and the life" (11:25)—*eternal* life—which comes into the world exclusively through Jesus the Messiah, whom John reveals to be none other than the divine *Logos* made flesh (1:1, 14).

Clement of Alexandria (c. 150–c. 215) had this to say about the composition of the Gospel of John: "Last of all, aware that the *physical* facts had been recorded in the

Gospels, encouraged by his pupils and irresistibly moved by the Spirit, John wrote a *spiritual* gospel."[1] Clement makes a distinction between the "physical" or "fleshly" nature of the other Gospels and the "spiritual" nature of John. By this he doesn't mean that the others are of negligible worth, but that they deal with outer matters and events, recording the *ipsissima verba* (the "true words") of Christ, while John goes deeper, plumbing the otherwise concealed profundities of Christ's meaning and purpose, presenting his hearers with the *ipsissima vox* (the "true voice") of Christ. It's an idea that seems more credible when one considers a saying of Jesus that appears in both Matthew (11:27) and Luke (10:22), often referred to as the "bolt from the Johannine blue": "All things were delivered to me by my Father; and no one knows the Son except the Father, and neither does anyone know the Father except the Son and anyone to whom the Son wishes to reveal him." This text might even be said to summarize the message of the Gospel of John — *although here it is in two of the Synoptic Gospels* (we may recall, too, that at the center of the Gospel of Mark is the Transfiguration, *in which the Father reveals the Son*). All one need do is compare the following verses in John to see the similarities with Matthew 11:27 and Luke 10:22 above: John 3:35; 7:29; 10:15; 13:3; 17:2.

There is another reason that John may have been considered the "spiritual" Gospel. It indirectly alludes to its own inspiration as the *memory* of Jesus's words by way of the Paraclete, who is identified by Christ as the Holy Spirit. "Paraclete" (παράκλητος, "*paráklētos*") means "one who comes alongside," "strengthener," "encourager," or "advocate." The same word is used to describe Jesus in 1 John 2:1.[2] In the Gospel, Jesus says: "These things I have spoken to you, while I am still with you. But the

---

[1] Eusebius, *Ecclesiastical History*, VI, 14; emphasis added.
[2] "My little children, I am writing this to you so that you may not sin; but if any one does sin, we have an advocate [παράκλητον] with the Father, Jesus Christ the righteous..."

Counselor [*paráklētos*], the Holy Spirit, whom the Father
will send in my name, he will teach you all things, and
bring to your remembrance all that I have said to you (14:25–
26; emphasis added). The implication here, of course, is
that the Spirit is teaching and reminding the hearers of
Jesus's words *through this very Gospel*. It suggests that the
long monologues of Jesus in John, so unlike the sayings
in the Synoptics, and often difficult to distinguish from
the narrator's voice (note the third chapter, for example),
are spiritually inspired expansions of original sayings of
Jesus, the authenticity of which—despite the great heaps
of distrustful academic criticism of modern times, which
has become both a kind of self-perpetuating "orthodoxy"
and an industry—need not be doubted.

These are not merely expansions, however, but expansions both profoundly mystical and cleverly literary in
their Greek rendering. John's poetic use of simple Greek
vocabulary would certainly have delighted a Hellenic
audience. As Greek writing goes, the Gospel is remarkably
unpretentious, and yet the mystical layers of the text seem
sometimes to be endless. Leon Morris, the Australian
biblical commentator, is accredited with having remarked
somewhere that John's Gospel is "shallow enough that a
child may wade and deep enough that an elephant can
swim." As I noted in my book, *The Woman, the Hour, and
the Garden: A Study of Imagery in the Gospel of John*,

> the Gospel of John is not a work of theology in any
> rationalistic sense. It is not a work of linearity and
> systematic logic. Its doctrines are not encased in hard-
> and-fast terms; and its imagery and language are *poetic*.
> As poetic, the language adopted is also *intentionally
> ambiguous* at times (this is a vital point, as we shall
> see). It is *theology* in the mystical and contemplative
> sense of that word. It is a "testimony" .... It is about
> "truth" (*aletheia*), which is not *simply* to be understood
> as biographical accuracy or historical detail. Historical
> and biographical information are certainly present,

providing the framework of the book. But the Gospel of John, in its final shape, is a *poetic work* with a *carefully chosen vocabulary* that holds the key to its deepest meaning. Understand the language, the vocabulary, and "the doors of perception" will be "cleansed"...

John displays remarkable skill for using Greek words effectively, a fact already recognized in the early third century by Origen. He understood John to be a proficient theologian, taking great care with his artful use of language. Notably, John makes the most of metaphors (for example, bread, light, door, shepherd, resurrection, road, vine), and of the multiple meanings contained in a number of Greek words (e.g., *logos* [which can mean "word," "message," and "reason"], *doxa* [which can mean both "glorious radiance" and "praise"], and *ano* [which can mean both "again" and "from above"]).[3] If the latter are not "portmanteau" words, they are at least words that are portmanteaus of meaning—that is to say, each one is a "suitcase" full of various interpretive possibilities. It is probable that John would not have us choose *either* this meaning *or* that meaning with such words, but rather that we should take them and their host of meanings together—a sort of wordplay. So, for instance, *doxa* means *both* glory (radiance) *and* praise.[4] What we can justly call John's work of *literature* suggests to us that, although the author's and editors' first language may have been Aramaic and the frame of their minds Semitic, their choice of *Greek* words was brilliant and utterly unforgettable. In places the Johannine poetic vocabulary conjures up mythological themes from the earliest chapters of Genesis, in other places it is witty in its use of verbal ambiguity, and it always makes rich use of profound and multivalent metaphors. The poetic imagination is coupled

---

[3] Nicodemus's incomprehension in 3:4 concerning Jesus's use of *ano* is a wonderfully adroit play on the word.

[4] The passage comparing Isaiah to the Pharisees in 12:37–43 turns on the ambiguity of *doxa* as meaning both "praise" and "glory."

in John with an evident facility for Greek vocabulary, and the result is an enduring masterpiece of poetic prose.[5]

I will conclude this section of the chapter by noting the two sets of *seven* that are embedded in the structure of the Gospel. These are the seven "I am" statements of Jesus and the seven "signs" that Jesus performs. Seven was a sacred number, suggesting among other things, wholeness.[6]

In the "I am" sayings, Jesus indicates that he shares the divine nature of the Father (a point stated explicitly elsewhere in the Gospel: 1:1; 10:30; 20:28). "I am" was God's "name" as revealed to Moses in Exodus 3. The tetragrammaton, YHWH, was the third person pronoun of the sacred designation: "He is." Without commentary, then, here are the seven sayings: "I am the bread of life" (John 6:35, 41, 48, 51), "I am the light of the world" (John 8:12), "I am the door of the sheep" (John 10:9 ff.), "I am the good shepherd" (John 10:7, 9), "I am the resurrection and the life" (John 11:25), "I am the way, the truth, and the life" (John 14:6), and "I am the true vine" (John 15:1, 5).

---

[5] *The Woman, the Hour, and the Garden: A Study of Imagery in the Gospel of John* (Grand Rapids: Eerdmans, 2016), 9–10, 11–12.

[6] Seven is, of course, four plus three; likewise, twelve is four multiplied by three. As we saw in the first chapter when commenting on Irenaeus's defense of *four* canonical Gospels, four is associated with such created features as four corners of the earth and four winds. Three is associated with the three levels of earth, under the earth, and the heavens. Twelve not only is a multiple of these numbers, but its cosmic significance is also visible in the heavens with the twelve constellations (note the "twelve stars" mentioned Rev. 12:1, that crown the Woman clothed with the sun). It is the number, too, of the twelve tribes of Israel. Twelve and seven were emphasized when we briefly looked at Mark's account of the feeding of the five thousand. We noted there that the "twelve baskets" of fragments taken up had possible significance in relation to the Israelites. Similarly, we noted the seven baskets of fragments taken up after the feeding of the four thousand, with their possible link to the seventy nations of the gentiles. And, in Luke, Jesus not only has twelve disciples, but an additional seventy. These numbers all point to totality, fullness, and completeness. Thus, in John, seven "I am" statements and seven "signs" indicate that a definitive revelation of God has come into the world with Jesus.

Only John refers to Jesus's miracles as "signs," indicating that *they are meant to be interpreted*; they point to something more profound than the physical events described in the text. John provides seven such signs, which again I list without comment: Jesus changes water into wine (John 2:1–12), heals a nobleman's son (John 4:46–54), heals the lame man at the pool (John 5:1–11), feeds the five thousand (John 6:1–15), walks on the sea (John 6:16–21), heals the man born blind (John 9:1–12), and — at the center of the Gospel — Jesus raises Lazarus from the dead (John 11).

To conclude this first section of the chapter, I want to counter the longstanding but entirely wrongheaded notion that John's Gospel is an antisemitic book. The reasons for such an incorrect assumption are rooted in the sad history of Christian–Jewish relations. This Gospel and other New Testament texts (all written, it must be pointed out, by Jews) have been employed down the centuries first in anti-Judaic polemics and, subsequently, by hardened antisemites. This has been made worse by generations of translators, all of whom should have known better, who have repeatedly mistranslated the word Ἰουδαῖος ("*Ioudaios*") as "Jew" instead of "Judean." Here allow me to quote my brother, David Bentley Hart:

> [T]he Gospel of John has often been accused of anti-Semitism, despite the anachronism of the very concept. Where English readers are accustomed to reading the Gospel as referring, often opprobriously, to "the Jews," the original text is usually referring to the indigenous Temple and synagogue authorities of Judaea, or even as "Judaeans" as opposed to "Galileans" (see, for instance, 7:1). The Gospel definitely reflects the disenchantment of Jewish Christians in Asia Minor [where John's Gospel was most likely composed] with those they saw as having expelled them from the synagogue, and later Christian culture certainly often took this as an excuse for anti-Jewish violence and injustice, but it would be misleading to impute to the Gospel the sort of religious prejudices born in later generations . . . [7]

---

[7] *New Testament*, 2nd ed. (New Haven, 2023), 549–50.

Indeed, mistranslating a verse like John 7:1 in the way that most English translators have done renders the text absurd (the RSV, for instance: "After this Jesus went about in Galilee; he would not go about in Judea, because *the Jews* [οἱ Ἰουδαῖοι, "*hoi Ioudaioi*" = the Judeans] sought to kill him"; emphasis added). John 7 is clearly making a distinction *not* between Galileans and "Jews," but between Galileans and *Judeans*, in particular the Pharisaic authorities in Jerusalem. In John, there is a distinct emphasis on *regionalism*, which even elevates the spiritual acuity of *the Samaritans* over that of the Judeans. Chapter 4 has the Samaritans coming *en masse* to Jesus and (astoundingly enough) proclaiming him "the Savior of the world." Whereas even a perceptive Pharisee like Nicodemus had failed to understand Jesus's message and person in the third chapter, the Samaritans one chapter later see both clearly. John's castigation of "the Judeans" is a rebuke of the religious elite centered in Jerusalem: they, among all peoples, *should* have understood Jesus's revelation, according to the perspective of this Gospel, and yet they failed to do so. Jesus makes this point polemically more than once in the book. The Gospel of John, then, is not an anti-Jewish book any more than, say, the book of Jeremiah is, with its hard words against obdurate authorities, or the book of Jonah, with its caricature of an obstinate Hebrew prophet.

2.

Throughout the text, the Gospel of John employs "coded" language and images.[8] The church fathers and medieval doctors of the church, both Eastern and Western, following Clement of Alexandria — as we said

---

[8] In 2014, I was invited to contribute to Fr Al Kimel's blog, *Eclectic Orthodoxy*. The essay I contributed grew into a book — *The Woman, the Hour, and the Garden: A Study of Imagery in the Gospel of John* (Eerdmans, 2016). I have reproduced and updated that original 2014 essay here as the second section on John in this chapter. The book, of course, is richer and includes a good deal more material on the subject.

above — read John as a "spiritual Gospel," meaning that its message requires proper unveiling and interpretation within the assembly of believers. To that end, there are specific terms that John repeats in his writings, and analyzing these terms helps us discover half-hidden themes and analogies. I would like, then, in this short analysis to look at how John uses the word and image of "the Woman" in his Gospel. It is, I believe, a significant feature of his message. As I will suggest, it provides insight into how John's church appears to have understood its own identity. I begin near the end of the Gospel, at the foot of Christ's cross. Looking at select verses from John 19:25–42 below, the reader will see that I have put three words in italics. These are "Woman," "hour," and "garden."

> But standing by the cross of Jesus were his mother, and his mother's sister, Mary the wife of Clopas, and Mary Magdalene. When Jesus saw his mother, and the disciple whom he loved standing near, he said to his mother, "*Woman*, behold, your son!" Then he said to the disciple, "Behold, your mother!" And from that *hour* the disciple took her to his own home. After this Jesus, knowing that all was now finished, said (to fulfill the scripture), "I thirst."...They took the body of Jesus, and bound it in linen cloths with the spices, as is the burial custom of the Jews. Now in the place where he was crucified there was a *garden*, and in the *garden* a new tomb where no one had ever been laid. So because of the Jewish day of Preparation, as the tomb was close at hand, they laid Jesus there.

An astute reader of John will already know that the words "Woman" (γυνή, "*gyne*") and "hour" (ὥρα, "*hora*") show up in the Gospel at significant places in the text, sometimes in proximity to one another. Let us look at the passages where one or the other appears, or both appear together. The word "woman" in John doesn't always have a special significance, but whenever Jesus addresses someone as "Woman" in John, which he does three times (his mother, the Samaritan woman, and Mary Magdalene), it does. (I exclude 8:10 here, in which Jesus addresses the woman taken in adultery as "Woman." The entire passage in which the account appears, 7:53–8:11, appears to be a later addition to the Gospel. It's only for that reason I don't discuss it below. Still, the very fact that Jesus addresses her in this fashion may provide a clue as to how the passage found its way into John—and we should be thankful that it did and that it's undeniably canonical.) The word "hour" likewise doesn't always convey a special meaning, but when it appears in John, it has significance.

Here are the three instances in which Jesus addresses various women as "Woman," and note the mention of "hour" in the first two passages (in italics):

1. Jesus addresses his mother:

> Jesus also was invited to the marriage, with his disciples. When the wine failed, the mother of Jesus said to him, "They have no wine." And Jesus said to her, "*O Woman*, what have you to do with me? *My hour* has not yet come." (2:2–4)

2. Jesus addresses the Samaritan woman:

> Jesus said to her, "*Woman*, believe me, *the hour* is coming when neither on this mountain nor in Jerusalem will you worship the Father. You worship what you do not know; we worship what we know, for salvation is from the Jews. But *the hour* is coming, and now is when the true worshipers will worship the Father in spirit and truth, for such the Father seeks to worship him. (4:21–23)

3. Two angels and Jesus address Mary Magdalene outside the garden tomb, following Jesus's resurrection:

> But Mary stood weeping outside the tomb, and as she wept she stooped to look into the tomb; and she saw two angels in white, sitting where the body of Jesus had lain, one at the head and one at the feet. They said to her, "*Woman*, why are you weeping?" She said

to them, "Because they have taken away my Lord, and I do not know where they have laid him." Saying this, she turned round and saw Jesus standing, but she did not know that it was Jesus. Jesus said to her, "*Woman, why are you weeping? Whom do you seek?*" (20:11–15)

The first two instances above refer specifically to *Jesus's* "hour." Other texts in John also refer to it: 5:25–30; 7:30; 8:20; 12:23–28; 13:1; 16:32; and 17:1. Jesus also uses the word "time" — καιρός ("*kairos*") — in a way synonymous with "hour" in 7:6–8.

In addition to the above passages, we have, most crucially, Jesus's enigmatic words to his disciples in 16:21, which tie together the various references above, as we shall see. Here I will give my literal rendering of this text as it appears in Greek:

> When *the Woman* is in travail she has sorrow, because *her hour* has come; but when she is delivered of the child, she no longer remembers the anguish, for joy that a man [ἄνθρωπος, "*anthropos*"] is born into the world.

Two things should immediately strike us: First, the word "Woman" has a *definite article*; literally, it is "*the* Woman." Second, the "hour" mentioned is "*her* hour" — that is to say, *the hour referred to in this verse is the hour when the Woman gives birth.*

Keep those two points in mind, because we will come back to them.

The hour of Jesus's glorification in John is the "hour" of his crucifixion. With that event his mission in the world is "accomplished" (19:30). It is the source and spring of new life for mankind. It is the hour in which resurrection for all humanity can be said to begin, as well (see 5:25–26). The paradox is that *the hour of the cross* is the beginning of *our new birth* (see 3:3–8).

The enigmatic saying of Jesus in 16:21 presents us with a curious question: Is the *Woman's* "hour" the same as *Jesus's* "hour"? The answer, I suggest, is *yes*. "The Woman"

and Jesus share "the hour" of the cross, and in that hour
"the Woman" becomes the birthgiver of a new "*man*"
(*anthropos* = "human being"; not, as some translations
render it, a "child"). Going a step further, does the word
"Woman," when addressed to the three women in the
passages above (Jesus's mother, the Samaritan woman,
and Mary Magdalene), refer in a spiritual sense to *a single
image or archetype*? Is there an archetypal "Woman" in
relation to whom these three specific women stand as
types? Are these three women also "the Woman" of 16:21,
and, if so, what significance does that have for John, his
community, and for us?

Undoubtedly, the three women are to be understood
as three distinct persons. John doesn't tend toward flat
allegory. He is more subtle than that. All three women
are individuals, delicately delineated with psychologi-
cal insight. But I would also suggest that John has, with
implicit intent, put the word "Woman" on Jesus's lips in
his book, precisely in order to signify a specific *something
else* that we are meant to understand in his use of that
address, something common to all three that can be
glimpsed shining through each of these distinct persons
like refractions of a single light.

So, what might the importance of "Woman" be as an
address? It has bothered any number of pious exegetes,
for example, that Jesus addresses his mother in John 2
in this seemingly discourteous way. After all, this is his
mother. Surely, we wouldn't address our own mothers in
this fashion; and if we are Orthodox, Catholics, Angli-
cans, or Christians of any other tradition in which Mary
holds an exalted place, we can't imagine Jesus speaking
to her so disrespectfully. But all those considerations miss
John's likely intent. This Gospel, we may recall, never
even divulges the name of Jesus's mother. Like "the disciple whom Jesus loved," she is never named. Something
else is going on here, although it clearly has an embryonic
relationship to later "Marian" piety.

There are just three possible ways to understand Jesus's address to his mother as "Woman": either (1) it was a "distancing" term, in order to prevent her from interfering in his high calling, or (2) it was some sort of endearment or respectful term for her, which we—coming as we do from a very different cultural context—have failed to recognize, or (3) the term has a *symbolic* purpose.

We can dismiss the first two possibilities outright. First, although the statement does indeed distance Jesus from his mother (literally, he says, "Woman, what is there between me and you?"), there is no justification for thinking the address was meant to be abrasive, dismissive, or rude. That he addresses her again in exactly the same fashion, while he is on the cross and seeing to her comfort and care after his departure from the world (19:26), should make it sufficiently evident that his use of "Woman" in John 2 isn't meant as rejection or belittlement. If its use isn't disrespectful in 19:26, then it's extremely unlikely that its use in 2:4 disrespectful. On the other hand, could he possibly have meant the address as the opposite of disrespect, as a sort of endearment? One plainly silly translation has in fact rendered it "dear lady"; and the Revised Standard Version, which I have used above, renders it politely as "O Woman." But there is no "O" in the original Greek verse, nor "dear," nor even the word "lady"; just "Woman." He is clearly not using the term as an endearment. We are left, then, with the third possibility: the Gospel means for us to infer something *symbolic*. And, if this is so for Jesus's mother, it seems probable that the same is true for both the Samaritan woman and Mary Magdalene as well.

So, then, how might these three women, when addressed as "Woman," be related to "the Woman" of 16:21? And what is it that the latter represents?

If we look at the immediate context of John 16:21, at the verses (20 and 22) that immediately precede and follow it, we note that Jesus is speaking to the disciples about the "sorrow" that *they — the disciples —* will undergo at his departure, and of the later joy that *they* will feel when they see him again: "Truly, truly, I say to you, you will weep and lament, but the world will rejoice; you will be sorrowful, but your sorrow will turn into joy" (vs. 20); "So you have *sorrow* now, but I will see you again and your hearts will rejoice, and no one will take your joy from you" (vs. 22). It is to speak to the feelings of sorrow that *the disciples* are to experience, that Jesus offers the parabolic image of the Woman in travail: "When the Woman is *in travail* she has *sorrow*, because her hour has come." The first thing to note, then, is that "the sorrow" and "joy" of "the Woman" are symbolic of the "sorrow" and "joy" that his disciples will experience. The second thing to note is that the Woman's travail is that of *childbirth*. She is bringing a new life into the world. It is the birth of "a man" (*anthropos*). To put it succinctly, "her hour" is the hour when she gives birth to a *new man*.

Who, then, is "the Woman"? If we consider the context in which the saying is presented, we see that the Woman (with her man-child) is directly identified with Christ's *disciples*. There is, in fact, every good reason to believe that "the Woman" and her man-child together comprise a single image of Jesus's (and John's) community of followers — that is to say, she represents the church.

Have we anything in the writings of John to suggest that the whole community of Jesus's followers was conceived of as "feminine" and symbolized as a "Woman" with offspring (i.e., baptized members)? Well, in fact, we have. In the Second Letter of John, we read the following:

> The elder to the elect lady and her children, whom I love in the truth, and not only I but also all who know the truth, because of the truth which abides in us and will be with us for ever: Grace, mercy, and peace will be with us, from God the Father and from Jesus Christ the Father's Son, in truth and love. I rejoiced greatly to find some of your children following the truth, just

> as we have been commanded by the Father. And now
> I beg you, lady, not as though I were writing you a
> new commandment, but the one we have had from
> the beginning, that we love one another. (2 John 1–5)

The same letter concludes with these words: "The children of *your elect sister* greet you" (2 John 13; emphasis mine).

The word translated "lady" in these verses is an honorific term, *kyria*. It is the feminine equivalent of "Lord" — *kyrios*. There seems little doubt that the "elect lady" and her "children" represent the community to whom "the elder" is writing in 2 John, and "the children of your elect sister" is a reference to the members of the local church from which he writes: these are, spiritually understood, two "ladies" — two churches — who are surrounded by the children to whom they have given spiritual birth (through baptism). The "icon" or image of the community, it seems, was that of a Woman, a "lady" with her offspring gathered about her. In addition, it appears that each church was seen as a "sister" among "sisters," each with her own children. Each community was dignified as a "lady" and regarded as a "sister" of equal dignity with all the rest. It's likely that the reason for the high title, *kyria,* was due to the spiritual union each church shared with its *Kyrios.* The "children" of the "elect lady" and her "elect sister," one may safely assume, were the baptized communicants.

That the church continued to be symbolized as a virgin bride and mother through the millennia is well known. One is reminded of Paul's words to the Christian community in Corinth, in 2 Corinthians 11:2, in which the word "you" is plural: "I feel a divine jealousy for you, for I betrothed you as a pure bride [literally, 'virgin'] to her one husband." We find it, for instance, in other very early Christian writings. For example, *The Shepherd of Hermas,* which was written in Rome in the second century, depicts the church as an ancient lady who grows ever younger through a series of visions. Nor can one truly appreciate

patristic and medieval devotion to the Blessed Virgin
Mary without understanding that she — the Virgin and
Mother who literally gave birth to the physical "body
of Christ" — was viewed from the earliest centuries as
the foremost icon of the church, the spiritual "body of
Christ." The church was viewed as both "virginal" (that
is, holy in essence) and as the "mother" of the baptized.
Numerous texts of the fathers and later writers, East and
West, amply illustrate this connection between Mary and
the church. It should not be difficult for us to recognize
the seeds of this spiritual insight already in John's writings,
and that "the Woman" in travail is an image of Jesus's
first community of followers.

Pressing further, it is not too much of a leap to assume
that "the Woman" also alludes to the first and archetypal
Woman of Genesis: "And Adam said, 'this now is bone
of my bones, and flesh of my flesh; she shall be called
woman [*gyne*], because she was taken out of her husband'"
(Gen. 2:23; LXX). Following the account of the Fall in
Genesis 3, God speaks first to the serpent, then to the
woman, and finally to Adam in response to what has
occurred earlier in the same chapter. It is God's words to
the woman that are particularly relevant: "I will greatly
multiply your pains and your groaning; in pain you shall
bring forth children" (Gen. 3:17). John 16:21 appears to
echo these words of Genesis: "When the Woman is in
travail she has sorrow." A few verses later in Genesis 3,
we read in the Greek version: "And Adam called the
name of his wife 'Life' [ζωή, "*Zoe*"], because she was
the mother of all the living [ζώντων, "*zonton*," meaning
those possessing *Zoe*]" (Gen. 3:21). We should take special notice here of the Greek name or title given to the
woman (Eve) — "*Zoe*" ("Life") — and of the designation
of her children — "*zonton*" ("living").

With that Greek name, "*Zoe*," we in fact have the very
word that John uses exclusively to indicate *eternal life*.
John uses the other two Greek words in his writings that

mean "life" (*psyche* and *bios*), but, whenever he and other New Testament writers refer specifically to "*eternal* life," the word for "life" is *zoe*. Perhaps, then, there is a deeper significance to the image of "the Woman" in John 16:21. We might reasonably conjecture that whenever the word *zoe*—"eternal life"—was cited in the context of John's churches, the hearers also heard an echo of the name given to the first woman.

To be clear, I am not saying that the women in John (Christ's mother, the Samaritan Woman, and Mary Magdalene) are mere symbols for an abstract concept, in this case, "eternal life." That would mean forcing an allegorical meaning onto an idea that is multivalent, subtle, and poetic in nature. The message of the Gospel of John relies on the use of metaphor, suggestion, and imagery. What I mean to say is that "Woman" in these specific texts is intended to conjure up a multivalent image, one which is, all at once and intertwined, the archetypal first woman as "mother" and giver of "life" (*zoe*-life, that is), the community of Christ's "reborn" followers, and the restoration of God's life to human beings which comes through the resurrected Christ and through the *ekklesia* that is "wed" to him. John is not a dry "systematic" theologian; he is poetically consistent and therefore mystically coherent. So, in one place the mother of Jesus can be "the Woman," in another it is the Samaritan woman who reflects this image, and in another, it is Mary Magdalene. There is, however, only one archetypal "Woman" towards whom this form of address always points, who stands above and behind them all, but there are three distinct women thus addressed. In each instance, what Jesus says to these women determines the significance of the allusion, and the context of each statement is also relevant.

Let me illustrate what I mean.

The first, and arguably most important, person Jesus calls "Woman" is his mother in 2:1–12. Jesus and his disciples attend a wedding at Cana. The wine runs out, and his mother draws his attention to the fact: "They have no wine." His response, literally rendered, is this: "What is between me and you, Woman? My hour has not yet come" (2:4). Apparently, she is not put off by Jesus's words to her. Undeterred, then, she responds by addressing the servants: "Whatever he tells you, do" (2:5). If she represents here, as I have indicated above, the Christian church, this would be an apt response—it is the sort of thing the church would say to her baptized "children." We know what comes next. Jesus changes a superabundance of water into a superabundance of wine, which is his first "sign," and the result is that "his disciples believed in him" (2:11). We wish only to note here the enigmatic statement of Jesus to his mother: "What is there between me and you, Woman?" and his designation of the hour that hasn't yet arrived as "my hour."

Bearing this in mind, we recall next that in 16:21 "the Woman" in travail rejoices when she brings an *anthropos* into the world. In that verse, we are told that the time of giving birth is "*her* hour." So, then, in 2:4 we have two notable emphases: "my hour," and the question, "What is between me and you?"—in other words, "What do we share in common?" Then, in 16:21, we hear of "the Woman" who gives birth at "*her* hour." Lastly, turning to 19:26–27, we read about Jesus on the cross (significantly, near a *garden*—verse 41). In this agonizing context, the following exchange transpires: "When Jesus saw his mother, and the disciple whom he loved standing near, he said to his mother, 'Woman, behold, your son!' Then he said to the disciple, 'Behold, your mother!' And from that hour the disciple took her to his own home." Again, we have the address "Woman," and again mention of an hour, but this time it isn't said to be either Jesus's or the Woman's hour singularly. Rather, it is "*that* hour."

To summarize, then, in 2:4, Jesus refers to "*my* hour"; in 16:21, the hour of the Woman giving birth is "*her* hour"; and now, in 19:27, the hour in which "the disciple whom

[Jesus] loved" took Jesus's mother—*now the disciple's mother too*—into his home is "*that* hour." It is, in other words, *the same hour* that is referred to in *all three instances*; and what is "between" Jesus and his mother—the Woman—is precisely the hour which is both Jesus's hour and her hour. It is the hour in which the mother gives birth to the new *anthropos*, who in turn is represented by the *beloved disciple* (the "founder" of the Johannine church, the exemplary disciple in the Gospel); and this beloved disciple is the first of many "children" who are to be gathered about "the lady." And this shared hour is indeed, as 16:21 said, an hour of sorrow and travail. The "mother of Jesus" is both the church and the "mother of all the [eternally] living," the true *Zoe*. Or, as later generations would put it, Mary is the second—or new—Eve.

And that brings us back to the garden. That all this happens at the cross, where a garden is located, is significant. As Christians from the earliest centuries recognized in this scene, the crucified Christ is revealed as the true Tree of Life, and the two standing at the foot of that Tree recapitulate the first human beings in the Garden of Eden. Genesis 3 is thus recapitulated, but this time the pair is given access to the Tree of Life.

Perhaps we may find the idea that the mother of Jesus is also the mother of Jesus's disciples difficult to grasp. If she represents, in the spiritual reading of the text, the community of Jesus's disciples (the church, the bride of the bridegroom as indicated in John 3:29), how can she also be his "mother"? Wouldn't it be more likely that she represents Israel, the Old Testament church, and not the New Testament church? But that is not only to miss the fluidity of metaphor but also to draw too sharp a distinction between the Old Testament church and the New Testament church—something first-century Christians did not do. For them, the "church" had its origin in the very beginning, with the first pair in Eden. It was reconstituted, after failure upon failure, with the calling

of Abraham (Gen. 12). From the perspective of the New
Testament — and of John — a disjuncture between the
Old Testament *ekklesia* and the *ekklesia* of Christ is not
clear or obvious. The book of Revelation, for example,
describes the vision of "a Woman clothed with the sun"
who is "with child" and "cried out in pangs of birth"
(see Gen. 3:17 and John 16:21). Her child is Christ, who
will rule all nations and who is "caught up to God and
to his throne." The woman then flees into the wilderness
to escape the dragon (who is Satan, the "ancient serpent"
of Eden; 12:9). Lastly, we are told, "the dragon was angry
with the woman, and went off to make war on the rest of
her offspring, on those who keep the commandments of
God and bear testimony to Jesus" (Rev. 12:1–2, 5–6, 9, 13,
17; emphasis mine). Here, in a single symbolic Woman,
we have both the "mother" of Jesus and the "mother" of
other offspring — those who are, in fact, Jesus's disciples.
In the mind of the writer of the book of Revelation, no
clear distinction exists between Israel (the mother of
Jesus) and the church (the mother of Jesus's disciples).
They are, spiritually, one and the same "Woman."

Turning briefly, then, to the other two women whom
Jesus addresses as "Woman" in John's Gospel, we note
first his words to the Woman of Samaria: "Woman,
believe me, the hour is coming when neither on this
mountain nor in Jerusalem will you worship the Father."
He goes on to say that the hour is coming "when the true
worshipers will worship the Father in spirit and truth"
(cf. John 4:21–24). That is to say, "true worshipers" will
gather from all places, Jews and Gentiles both, and share
in "spirit and truth" together as one community. There
will be no division between Jews, Samaritans, Greeks
(12:20–22), and those who come from other nations. To
this seemingly lowly Samaritan woman, with whom he
has discussed such high matters, Jesus reveals himself to
be the Messiah (4:25–26). She promptly goes and proclaims to her countrymen, "Come, see a man who told

me all that I ever did. Can this be the Christ?" (4:29) The Samaritans then come and listen to Jesus's word. "They said to the woman, 'It is no longer because of your words that we believe, for we have heard for ourselves, and we know that this is indeed the Savior of the world'" (4:42). The Samaritan woman, then, resembles "the lady" of 2 John, with her "children following the truth" (2 John 4). Although she is a Samaritan and outside the people of the Jews, she is nevertheless an apt type of that "church" which transcends "in spirit and truth" all such racial and national distinctions and has its origins in *Zoe*, "the mother of all the living," the first mother of all human beings and peoples.

Turning lastly to the scene in John 20 with Mary Magdalene, we have an even more striking reminder of Eden. Jesus's crucifixion and tomb are situated in a garden: "Now in the place where he was crucified there was a garden, and in the garden a new tomb where no one had ever been laid" (19:41). The cross is the true Tree of Life. From it comes *zoe*-life, symbolized by Jesus's spirit (breath), blood, and water (19:30, 34). When Jesus rises from the dead, he does so in the garden, and it is there that Mary encounters him and mistakes him for the gardener. "Woman," says Jesus to her, "why are you weeping? Whom do you seek?" (20:15). With these words we have a reversal of Genesis 3:9: "And [Adam and his wife] heard the voice of the Lord God walking in the garden in the afternoon; and both Adam and his wife hid themselves from the face of the Lord God in the midst of the trees of the garden" (LXX). Instead of the Lord God seeking for Adam and his wife, we have Mary Magdalene seeking for the supposedly mislaid or stolen body of Jesus. When she tries to hold him, Jesus says to her, "Do not hold me, for I have not yet ascended to the Father; but go to my brethren and say to them, 'I am ascending to my Father and your Father, to my God and your God'" (20:17). Up to this point in John's Gospel, Jesus had referred to the

Father as his Father, not "our Father." With this affirming statement made to Mary, he opens wide the door to fully restored union with God — his disciples can now share in his relationship with his God and Father. Jesus is saying, in effect, that he is "my Father — *and your Father too*, my God — *and your God too*."

The expulsion from the *Garden* in Genesis 3 is undone in this *garden*, and the message is conveyed through "the Woman" to the community of his disciples. We are then told that Mary, just as the Samaritan woman had gone to her countrymen, "went and said to the disciples, 'I have seen the Lord'" (20:18). Once again, we have "the lady" who gathers together the "children," this time emerging from the garden in which she was first seeking and then walking with the Lord.

Let me sum up all that we have seen above as simply as I can:

1. "The Woman" in travail in John 16:21 is intended to remind us of (a) the first woman, called *Zoe* in the Greek version of the Old Testament, who is the "mother of all the living," and thus the mother of all peoples and the church; and (b) an "icon" of the community of Jesus (the church), and the same as "the lady" with her "children" in 2 John.

2. When Jesus calls his mother, the Samaritan Woman, and Mary Magdalene "Woman," he is associating them with "the Woman" of 16:21 and all that she symbolizes.

3.

As we noted above, at the center of John's Gospel is the raising of Lazarus, with 11:38–44 at the very crux of the narrative. To understand the significance of this last and crowning "sign" of the seven in the Gospel, we should keep in mind the exchange between Jesus and Martha that precedes the event. When Jesus assures her that her "brother will rise again" (vs. 23), Martha quite naturally understands him to refer to the end (*eschaton*) of the age: "I know that he will rise again in the resurrection at the last day" (vs. 24). To this, Jesus responds with the fifth of his seven "I am" statements: "I am the resurrection and the life; he who believes [trusts] in me, though he die, yet shall he live, and whoever lives and believes [trusts] in me shall never die. Do you believe [trust] this?" (vss. 25–26). Here, in this brief exchange, what we have implicitly is the idea that the fulfillment — the end of the age — is *already present* or "realized" in Jesus. The words Jesus speaks in this passage can be viewed as a corrective to a strictly future-focused eschatology; the "end of history" isn't far off, it's *right here, now.*

The question directed to Martha, then, is also intended for the reader: "Do you have faith — i.e., will you *trust* — in this?" Many of us are so familiar with this passage and others in the New Testament that present the idea of "realized eschatology," that we sometimes fail to appreciate just how *early* in the church's history eschatology had been transformed among followers of Jesus. It can be found in the earliest layer of the New Testament, in the letters of Paul. I have become increasingly skeptical of the notion that this development was merely the result of the "delay" of Jesus's return in glory. "Realized eschatology" appears to be present in embryo form in the earliest decades of the church's existence. What ensued after Jesus's resurrection was a dawning realization that every hitherto "normal" expectation, every perception of what was "natural," and indeed the cosmos itself had been suddenly and forever altered. "The end" *had begun* and was *now unfolding* within the destined course of history. Indeed, *all* the evidence suggests that the church's earliest liturgies were celebrations of this very realization. The driving purpose behind the composition of the Gospel of John, understood in this light, was articulated well by the Jesuit theologian and church historian, Jean Daniélou. It is the view to which I subscribe without reservation, given that the Gospel was composed for the sake of those already baptized and participating in the liturgical and sacramental practices of the church.[9] Danielou writes: "If we must go back to the most ancient origin of treatises on *the symbolism of worship* [emphasis added], we should, perhaps, begin with the Gospel of St. John, if it is, as Oscar Cullmann believes, a kind of paschal catechesis commenting on the mysteries of Christ in relation to their biblical prefigurings and also to their prolongation in the sacraments."[10] In the exchange between Jesus and Martha, then, we see a solely future-focused eschatology, like an egg, cracking open ("I know that he will rise again in the resurrection on the last day") and "realized eschatology" breaking through the fragmentation of its shell ("I am the resurrection and the life...do *you* have faith in this?").

In such texts as 3:5 ("Truly, truly, I say to you, unless one is born of water and the Spirit, he cannot enter the kingdom of God"), 6:35 ("I am the bread of life"), and 15:1 ("I am the true vine"), we have unmistakable references to baptism and the Eucharist. We can hear this echoed in the words of 1 John 1:3: "That which we have seen and heard we proclaim also to you, so that you may have fellowship [communion] with us; and our fellowship [communion] is with the Father and with his Son Jesus Christ." John's emphasis is on an actual, not

---

[9] We should be very dubious about claims that the early church's worship was like the meetings of a "supper club" (as one recent and rather imbecilic interpretation has described it), or relaxed and disorganized. All the extant evidence from the NT and other first- and second-century writings makes it clear that early Christian worship was supervised, perhaps loosely hierarchical in structure but certainly hierarchical, sacramental, and liturgical—though, of course, the worship was not as elaborate or uniform as it was in later developments.

[10] Jean Daniélou, SJ, *The Bible and the Liturgy* (Ann Arbor, 1956), 8. Daniélou is citing O. Cullmann, *Urchristentum und Gottesdienst*, 2nd ed. (1950), 38–115.

just figural, "regeneration." It is not an act of "adoption." The baptized person lives simultaneously on two planes in this age. He or she is living an earthly, timebound life that must inevitably undergo all the infirmities and eventually the death of mortals, but simultaneously possesses the immortal life of the coming age. Put differently, the Christian is already *resurrected* "in spirit" with Jesus (to be "reborn" is the same thing in John as to be "resurrected"; we see the same idea in other NT texts outside the Johannine writings, of course — e.g., Colossians 3:1–4 and 2 Peter 1:4). "Eternal life" or "the life of the (coming) Age" is what Jesus brings into the cosmos by "becoming flesh" and — literally translated — "pitching his tabernacle among us" (ἐσκήνωσεν ἐν ἡμῖν, "*eskēnōsen en hēmin*"; 1:14). We see this as early as 1:4: "In him was life [*zoe*], and the life [*zoe*] was the light of men" (ἐν αὐτῷ ζωὴ ἦν, καὶ ἡ ζωὴ ἦν τὸ φῶς τῶν ἀνθρώπων), and the theme of Jesus as the giver of immortal "life" is stressed throughout the Gospel, culminating with the author's summary of his purpose in writing it in 20:31: "that you may believe [trust] that Jesus is the Christ, the Son of God, and that believing [trusting] you may have life in his name" (ἵνα πιστεύοντες ζωὴν ἔχητε ἐν τῷ ὀνόματι αὐτοῦ).

John is bold to assert that this trusting, new state of living — immortal and everlasting in scope — precludes hopelessness or a necessary dread of the judgment of God (Paul affirms something similar in Romans 8:1). One should be careful to construe John's claims correctly here: John is *not* saying that one *cannot* fall back into a condition of justifiable fear and shame before God (see 1 John 2:28), but rather that a life now lived in ongoing *faithfulness* (i.e., one of continuing trust — "do *you* have *faith* in this?") in Jesus — the source of eternal life — has set before it no threat of the future judgment. (This would seem to be in contrast with the parable of the sheep and goats in Matthew 25, although one might note that the "sheep" in that parable avoid condemnation on similar grounds to those John indicates in the verses quoted directly below.) The most straightforward text regarding this is 5:24–29, part of a monologue Jesus delivers to the "Judeans" who oppose him for (ironically) curing a lame man on a Sabbath day:

> Truly, truly, I say to you, he who hears my word and believes him who sent me, has eternal life; *he does not come into judgment*, but has passed from death to life. Truly, truly, I say to you, the hour is coming, and now is, when the dead will hear the voice of the Son of God, and those who hear will live. For as the Father has life in himself, so he has granted the Son also to have life in himself, and has given him authority to execute judgment, *because he is the Son of man*. Do not marvel at this; for the hour is coming when all who are in the tombs will hear his voice and come forth, those who have done good, to the resurrection of life, and those who have done evil, to the resurrection of judgment. [emphasis added]

The italicized words in the passage above have as their background passages in the book of Daniel and other apocalyptic literature. Jesus identifies himself as "the Son of Man" (see Daniel 7:13–14, in which "the Ancient of Days" bestows authority on the "one like a son of man"). This was a designation which originally simply meant "man" (for example, Ezekiel is addressed by God as "son of man" frequently in the book that bears his name). Later the title came to refer to the coming Messianic king (see the aforementioned reference in Daniel; this title appears also in such intertestamental books as *1 Enoch* and *2 Esdras*). It is with the Messianic figure that Jesus identifies himself in John 5. He is the One who has been granted the power to judge the world, he claims; those who "hear" his message and exercise faithfulness to God have nothing to fear from him (and we might well surmise that "faithfulness to God" would naturally embrace such charitable responsibilities as those enumerated in Matthew 25:31–46). Later, Jesus will declare that "now" — meaning the "hour" of his death and resurrection — has come the true judgment of the world: "Now is the judgment of this world, now shall the ruler of this world be cast out; and I, when I am lifted up from the earth, will draw all [πάντας] to myself" (12:31–32; RSV, slightly altered [11]). In the apparent failure of Jesus (when he is lifted up on the cross to die), in other words, he will draw *all* to himself, and — with him — *all* will be resurrected.

It is important to remember that in the Christian tradition, Jesus is not regarded as having risen from the dead *alone*. When he rose, all humanity rose along with him. Looking back, then, 5:25 quoted above, we can understand a little better what Jesus is inferring when he says, "Truly, truly, I say to you, the hour is coming, *and now is*, when the dead will hear the voice of the Son of God, and those who hear will live." And it is in the raising of Lazarus that the meaning of Jesus, as John presents it, comes into sharper focus.

Lazarus's resurrection foreshadows "the hour…when the dead will hear the voice of the Son of God, and those who hear will live." It exemplifies Jesus's authority over death itself. Lazarus is called from the dust of the tomb (reminding one, perhaps, of Adam being created from the clay of the earth), and he has need only to be unbound (11:44). He represents both the "all" that Jesus "draws to himself," and — spiritually — those baptized and "reborn." The raising of Lazarus also stands in John's Gospel as the final (the seventh) "sign" that Jesus gives. Paradoxically, it is this bestowal of life that sets things in motion in this Gospel for Jesus's death (11:45–57). And yet — paradox upon paradox — it is through his death ("lifting up") and what follows that he bestows life.

---

[11] The RSV has "all *men*" where the Greek simply has "all." It may be the case that John was implying "all human beings," but he could just as easily have meant "all creation."

4.

I briefly mentioned above that John has a facility for
what we might call, almost flippantly, "wordplay," but is
in fact a quality much more profound. He demonstrates
a poetic sensibility that makes ample use of the Greek
vocabulary to express as comprehensively as possible the
mystery of Christ's person. He is, as we have indicated,
writing for those within the church, who have been baptized and are participating in its worship and practice. At
the Gospel's outset, for instance, he employs the term
Logos (usually translated as "Word"), *which had already long*
been used to denote a "divine principle" or intermediary
through whom God creates and orders the cosmos. This
word — as multivalent in its meaning as the word *Tao* is
in Chinese — was used in the metaphysics of the Stoics,
among others; and the Alexandrian Hellenistic Jewish
thinker, Philo (c. 25 BC–c. AD 50) adopted it and even
referred to the *Logos* as God's "Son." In other words, by
using the term John was picking up on something that
was a recognizable feature in Greco-Roman and Hellenistic Jewish philosophical thought. In the latter context,
it was conceptually related to the depiction of personified
"Wisdom" in Proverbs, the Wisdom of Solomon, the
book of Sirach (Ecclesiasticus), and other sacred texts.
John's originality is in identifying this concept with the
historical man, Jesus, and explicitly calling both Jesus
and the eternal "Word" he "enfleshes" *Theos* — "God"
(1:1; see 20:28). There is a boldness in this identification
that would have been unanticipated, even alarming, for
those hearing it for the first time.

John "rings the changes" with other Greek words, as
well, drawing from them meanings that are not reducible to "either/or" but are best heard as "both/and." For
example, he plays on the word ἄνω ("*ano*") in Chapter 3,
in the dialogue between Jesus and Nicodemus, "a [reli-
gious] ruler of the Judaeans." The word ἄνω can mean both
"above" and "again," and in John's Gospel, it evidently

means *both* simultaneously. When Jesus tells Nicodemus that he must be "born *from above*" (γεννηθῇ ἄνωθεν, "*gennēthei anothen*"), the latter understands him to mean "born *again*": Nicodemus asks, "How can a man be born when he is old? Can he enter a *second time* into his mother's womb and be born?" (3:4; emphasis added). Jesus patiently explains that he is referring to a *higher* kind of birth, "that which is born of the flesh is flesh, and that which is born of the Spirit is spirit" (3:6). Whether Nicodemus's question is ironic or not, Jesus redirects his attention from biology to God's "breath" of life or creative "wind" *sent from above* (3:8; see Gen. 1:2). Nicodemus's incomprehension provokes Jesus to say, "Are you [the] teacher of Israel, and yet you do not understand this?" (3:10). We must come back to this Judean teacher's incomprehension, but first note that John, in constructing this dialogue in Greek, is playing on the different meanings of ἄνω, whereas Greek is a language that, presumably, Jesus and Nicodemus might not actually have employed in that context.

Nicodemus's incomprehension is contrasted with the receptiveness of the Samaritans in the next chapter, who say: "[W]e have heard for ourselves, and we know that this is indeed the Savior of the world" (4:42). In other words, whereas a Judean ruler was slow to understand, the people of another region and of mixed race, holding to the wrong form of religion, grasped the truth of who Jesus was. Further, in 4:45, the people in the region of Galilee "welcome him"; and in 7:1, he "walks about" in Galilee because, in the region of Judea, the Judeans (Ἰουδαῖοι) — meaning especially the religious rulers — are "seeking to kill him." The point, of course, is that the peoples of other regions (including "Greeks," as we will see below) had greater understanding of the mystery of his person than the religious rulers headquartered in Judea.

The comparative receptivity of the Galileans is also one of the instances in which John differs somewhat from the Synoptic Gospels. For example, early in his Gospel,

Luke describes an incident in which the people of Jesus's hometown in Galilee, outraged by his teaching, attempt to throw him off a cliff (Luke 4:28–30). John, on the other hand, avoids showing any other regional peoples — including the Galileans and Samaritans — in their worst light, with the single exception of the Judeans. The latter, by implication, should have recognized and confessed Christ. John frequently underscores the opposition of the religious authorities to Jesus. Only Nicodemus and Joseph of Arimathea are shown in a good light.

Another example of wordplay (for lack of a better term) is in John 12:20–50, and it also picks up on the theme of the Judeans' rejection of Christ. The word in question is δόξα ("*doxa*" = "glory"), which can refer to glory in the sense of "radiance" and glory in the sense of "praise." It can also mean to "appear" or to "seem." But it is the ambiguity of glory in its meanings of "radiance" and "praise" that John utilizes when contrasting the boldness exhibited by the priest and prophet, Isaiah (who, according to one tradition, was martyred — see below), with the pusillanimity of the Judaean religious authorities.

This lengthy passage is a summary of the Gospel's message up to this point. With Chapter 13, the book moves into the Passion narrative. What triggers the words of Jesus and the author's commentary in 12:20–50 is the arrival on the scene of "some Greeks." What immediately preceded their coming were the events of Jesus's raising of Lazarus from the dead (Chapter 11), the plotting of "the Judeans" to kill both Jesus and Lazarus (12:10–11), Mary of Bethany's anointing of Jesus's feet (12:1–11), and the entry of Jesus into Jerusalem on a foal (12:12–19). The verses 12:18–19 remind us once again of the Pharisees' animosity toward him: "The reason why the crowd went to meet him was that they heard he had done this sign [of raising Lazarus]. The Pharisees then said to one another, 'You see that you can do nothing; look, the world has gone after him.'" And *then — immediately after the alarmed Pharisees say that "the*

world has gone after him" — *as if to underscore that very point,*
Greeks show up. The implication is that not only have
Galileans, crowds of common people from Judea, and
the hated Samaritans "gone after him," but now even the
gentiles are seeking to come to him. (Some commentators
suggest that "Greeks" in this case refers to Hellenistic
Jews; but this seems unlikely from the context, where
"the world" in verse 19 strongly implies ethnicities from
outside the Hebrew context, and Jesus's words in verse
32 back up this interpretation: "[A]nd I, when I am lifted
up from the earth, will draw all [peoples] to myself.")

The Greeks approach "Philip, who was from Bethsaida
in Galilee," presumably because "Philip" is a Greek name
(and, possibly, he spoke Greek). Philip goes and gets
Andrew — another disciple who bears a Greek name —
and both go directly to Jesus with the request.[12]

Jesus's "answer" doesn't on the surface appear to
address the Greeks' wish to "see Jesus." Instead, his reply
is cryptic, which is a constant feature of John's Gospel. He
speaks of "the hour" of his coming death, using the metaphor of sown seed. He renews his call to self-sacrificial
discipleship (there is no other kind — the disciple, as
we will see below, is one who *confesses* his trust in Jesus).
He then comes back to the theme of "the hour" (vs. 23),
asking aloud, "Now is my soul troubled. And what shall I
say? 'Father, save me from this hour'? No, for this purpose
I have come to this hour" (vs. 27). A voice from heaven
responds, *which only Jesus can interpret.* To everyone else, it
sounds like thunder or perhaps "an angel speaking" (vss.
28–29). The voice declares, speaking to Jesus: "I have
glorified [your name], and I will glorify it again." Jesus
then proclaims: "Now is the judgment of this world, now

---

[12] As an aside, the fact that "Andrew" is a *Greek* name, while
"Simon," Andrew's brother, bears a *Jewish* one, calls into question
the assumption that Jesus and his disciples could have known no
Greek. The two cultures existed side by side, trading with and
otherwise influencing each other on a daily basis.

shall the ruler of this world be cast out" (vs. 31). In other words, "the future judgment" is being accomplished *now*, in the "hour" when he is to be "lifted up from the earth" (vs. 32). *In this is the answer to the Greeks*: I "will draw all [peoples] to myself"—tearing them away, that is, from the domination of "the ruler of this world." This isn't a "judgment," then, of people's consciences and deeds, but a judgment upon that usurping being who has brought "death" into the world (see Wisdom 2:24; Hebrews 2:14–15). (It is important to bear in mind that "death" is to be understood as simultaneously a bodily and spiritual reality, and the restoration of the latter is what will restore and transform the former.)

Those among the crowd respond to Jesus's words by asking about the Messianic "Son of Man": "We have heard from the law that the Christ remains for ever. How can you say that the Son of man must be lifted up? Who is this Son of man?" Jesus responds by exhorting them to walk in the light while the light (meaning himself) is still among them (see 9:4; 11:9–10). At this point, the narrator takes over the narrative in his own voice, revisiting themes that have been stated and restated throughout the Gospel up to this point. The chapter concludes with these words of Jesus:

> He who believes in me, believes not in me but in him who sent me. And he who sees me sees him who sent me. I have come as light into the world, that whoever believes in me may not remain in darkness. If any one hears my sayings and does not keep them, I do not judge him; for I did not come to judge the world but to save the world. He who rejects me and does not receive my sayings has a judge; the word that I have spoken will be his judge on the last day. For I have not spoken on my own authority; the Father who sent me has himself given me commandment what to say and what to speak. And I know that his commandment is eternal life. What I say, therefore, I say as the Father has bidden me. (12:44–50)

The Greeks, it seems, have been quite forgotten—unless, that is, one realizes that by their arrival *all the peoples of the world* (Jews, Samaritans, gentiles) have now emblematically been brought to Jesus in John's text.

Let us turn, then, to those earlier verses in which δόξα (*"doxa"*) — "glory" — appears (12:37–43), to see how John draws on two of its possible meanings. The italicized words in the passage below indicate where and how it is used:

> Though he had done so many signs before them, yet they did not believe in him; it was that the word spoken by the prophet Isaiah might be fulfilled:
>
> "Lord, who has believed our report, and to whom has the arm of the Lord been revealed?" [Isa. 53:1]
>
> Therefore they could not believe. For Isaiah again said, "He has blinded their eyes and hardened their heart, lest they should see with their eyes and perceive with their heart, and turn for me to heal them." [Isa. 6:10][13]
>
> Isaiah said this because he saw his [Jesus's] *glory* [= *radiance*] and spoke of him [see Isa. 6:1 ff.]. Nevertheless many even of the authorities believed in him, but for fear of the Pharisees they did not confess it, lest they should be put out of the synagogue: for they loved the *glory* [= "praise"] of men more than the *glory* [= both "praise" and "radiance"] of God.

It was the immortal, pre-incarnate, divine "radiance" (δόξα) of Christ that Isaiah had beheld in the Temple. With that in mind, we can better understand the reiteration of Jesus's declaration: "I have come as light [a *radiance*] into the world, that whoever believes in me may not remain in darkness" (vs. 45; cf. vss. 35–36; also 1:4; 8:12). That is to say, the *glory* that Isaiah beheld in its awe-inspiring, indeed frightening power, has been revealed

---

[13] There is no notion of "predestination" underlying this pronouncement in either Isaiah or John. Rather, it is the willful rejection—the refusal to hear and see revelation—that results in God's "blinding" and "hardening." It is, in a sense, the "natural" outcome of obduracy and "not having faith (trust)."

in the incarnate Son of Man, his divine radiance now veiled in flesh.

There is a subtle contrast in this passage between Isaiah, who *saw* and *confessed*, and those—including "rulers" who "had faith" but "who *did not confess* (as Isaiah had done)...lest they should be put out of the synagogue." As many commentators have noted, the threat of being cast out of the synagogue is a secondary theme in John (9:22; 16:2), perhaps indicating that the Christians of John's churches knew this threat firsthand in their context. Isaiah was also the prophet who had said the most about the inclusion of the gentiles among the people of God (see Isa. 42:6, for example, where a coming "light to the gentiles" is mentioned).

It appears that the pseudepigraphical writing, *The Ascension of Isaiah*, a complicated multi-layered text, may have some insight to provide. This fascinating book appears to be a work roughly contemporaneous with John's Gospel—written, it has been proposed, near the end of the first century. The original text seems to have been written in Hebrew. Later interpolations in the text reveal its influence among Christians. Its early chapters purport to tell how Isaiah came to be martyred. Of particular interest here is that an accusation of blasphemy is said to have been leveled at Isaiah for his alleged confession, "I have seen the LORD, and behold I am alive" (*Ascension of Isaiah* 3:9). Consequently, the prophet is "sawed in half with a wood saw" (*Ascension* 5:1–16; see Hebrews 11:37, which may be a reference to this legend).[14]

If John's remark that it was "fear" that caused many who had "believed" in Jesus to remain silent, not confessing the "glory" they had seen in him, it might be that this traditional story of Isaiah's boldness and martyrdom is in the background. The irony in the line, "they loved the

---

[14] *Ascension of Isaiah*; see: James H. Charlesworth, ed., *The Old Testament Pseudepigrapha*, *vol.* 2 (New York: 1985), 143 ff. Also known as *The Martyrdom of Isaiah*.

glory—praise—of men better than the glory—praise/
radiance—of God" is cutting indeed.

Isaiah went to his death, confessing the glory. Those
who fear to confess their faith in Jesus, even if it results
in their banishment or worse, are thus put to shame by
the bold example of that martyred prophet.

✣ ✣ ✣ ✣

All four canonical Gospels put demands on those who
take them to heart, just as Jesus was bold to make uncompromising demands on his disciples. Not one of the Gospels, humbly read with serious purpose, can be said to
make for "comfortable" reading. All four challenge the
reader and summon us to follow and obey Christ, the
Savior of the world. It is not for nothing that in three of
the four, Jesus explicitly calls those who would come after
him to take up the "cross" (as Bonhoeffer put it succinctly,
"When Christ calls a man, he bids him come and die"),
and John's parallel in 12:25–26 is no less exacting: "He
who loves his life loses it, and he who hates his life in this
world will keep it for eternal life. If any one serves me, he
must follow me; and where I am, there shall my servant
be also; if any one serves me, the Father will honor him."

And yet the Gospels reveal to observant "spiritual eyes"
both the glory and loving condescension of God, who
came to us in the flesh and showed his "face" in such a
fashion that human beings might comprehend it. In the
Gospels the promise remains, written in ancient texts
that are nonetheless alive and alight with holy fire: God
the Word became what we are so that, through him, we
might become what he is. We do not read them merely
to garner facts or accrue "evidence." The Gospels are at
once history made transparent to the timeless revelation
of God, and revelation enfleshed in the ebb and flow of
human history. There is no "historical Jesus" who isn't at
the same time "Christ our God." The Christian makes no
distinction between the two designations because—very
simply—there is no distinction to be made.

APPENDICES

The three appendices that follow are only tangentially related to the focus of this book, which is the four canonical Gospels, and only what I consider an assortment of "notes" on each. But I thought that a few supplements might be of interest and perhaps useful for readers. The first appendix deals with *The Gospel of Thomas*, which is, from among all the non-canonical Gospels, the one that has received the most attention; it has been called "the fifth Gospel" and—incorrectly, in my view—even assigned by some a first-century date. The second appendix is a thoroughly revised version of a chapter that first appeared in an earlier book of mine, *Strangers and Pilgrims Once More* (Eerdmans, 2014). It is a look at the whole canon of the Christian Bible (both the Old and New Testaments), which is the overall literary context in which the Gospels are situated and intentionally ordered as we find them: first Matthew, and *then* Mark, Luke, and John. The last appendix presents readers with *lectio divina*, "holy reading," the traditional way that scripture has been read within the Church.

APPENDIX 1
The Gospel of Thomas

I f we seek to understand *The Gospel of Thomas*, we must approach it cautiously. We should even be careful about referring to it as a "Gospel," since that term usually designates a *narrative* of Jesus's life, teachings, deeds, death, and resurrection — the stuff, in other words, that characterizes the canonical four. In the early centuries, quite a few Gospels were written — among them, *The Gospel of the Hebrews, The Gospel of Truth, The Gospel of Peter, The Gospel of Philip, The Gospel of the Egyptians, The Gospel of Mary (Magdalene), The Infancy Narrative of Thomas* (not to be confused with the work we will be discussing below), and so on. All of them were written later — usually, considerably later — than Matthew, Mark, Luke, and John. All of them are of historical interest, and a number of them reflect the doctrinal concerns of early Christian groups (some very much on the fringes). (Despite the current tendency of some to speak of differing "christianities," we should be more circumspect in our language. There were no "christianities" as such in the earliest centuries, but one emerging "Jesus tradition" with a wide variety of offshoots, some of which seem to have coalesced over time and some of which — the "Thomasine" tradition included — were either absorbed or disappeared entirely.)

What we refer to as *The Gospel of Thomas* could be more accurately referred to as "The Hidden Sayings of the Living Jesus Spoken to Thomas" or some such title, seeing that that is how its opening lines present its contents. (When we see the term "hidden," incidentally, we should assume that the text was intended to be read by those considered proficient enough in their understanding to interpret the meaning, metaphors, and allusions it contained.[1]) Nor should we take *The Gospel of Thomas*'s claim to be authentic — as coming from the "living Jesus" — at face value. The only extant version of the book we possess is not the original but a translation into Coptic, discovered at Nag Hammadi in Egypt in 1945, dating to the mid-fourth century. The original Greek text was composed earlier, and fragments of it, discovered at Oxyrhynchus in Egypt in 1897 and 1903, broadly date to circa 130–250. Some scholars have speculated that there may have been an even earlier Syriac text of *Thomas*, but if so, no trace of it has survived. The possibility exists that its origins may lie in Palestine, Syria, or Asia Minor and that the text was — at least, in its embryonic form — a Jewish-Christian sayings collection; the text's reverence for the authority invested in James the Just, the leader of the Jerusalem mother church, suggests as much.[2]

There are a few notable differences between the earlier Greek fragments and the later Coptic version of *Thomas*. What these textual discrepancies indicate is that the supposedly "complete" version we possess, which exists only in Coptic, is not only an occasionally awkward translation of the original Greek but a significantly edited version, apparently adjusted by unknown hands along doctrinal lines. This should alert readers that the Coptic Thomas *cannot* be fully trusted as it stands; it is *a late "unsteady" or "fluid" text that evolved and was altered — and possibly added to — over a long period of time*. That simple fact may

---

[1] For example, logion 7 — "Blessed is the lion which the man shall eat, and the lion become man; and cursed is the man whom the lion shall eat, and the lion become man" — is easier to understand when one knows that "lion" in ascetic Christian literature can refer either to the devil (not likely in this case) or to one's "animal passions" (much more likely in this instance). If the latter, it's a case of one's rational/spiritual "inner man" conquering the unruly desires and actions, rather than one being consumed by them.

[2] Logion 12: "The disciples said to Jesus: We know that thou wilt go from us. Who is he who shall be great over us? Jesus said to them: In the place to which you come, you shall go to James the Just for whose sake heaven and earth came into being."

disappoint those who have placed undue weight on the contents of the Nag Hammadi version (sometimes going so far as to regard that text as a more authentic source than our first-century canonical Gospels for understanding "the historical Jesus"(!), and sometimes seeing in it some forgotten wellspring of mystical insight that could somehow "reboot Christianity" in our own day). Still, given how much attention this admittedly fascinating text has received over the decades since its finding, it's worth our while to give it ours here, though briefly. Nor should the possibility be dismissed that, in addition to the parallel material it shares with the canonical Gospels in the first half of the text, it contains some hitherto unknown "sayings" that go back to Jesus. We shall see, too, that there is good reason to suspect that early Christian ascetics in Egypt (where both the Greek fragments and the Coptic text were discovered, significantly near the sites of two ancient Pachomian monasteries) found it spiritually valuable and — it's quite plausible — added their own touches to the text.

All told, *The Gospel of Thomas* contains 114 short sayings or "logia" (none of them exceeds 26 lines) and they can be categorized as follows. Some are *"proverbs, precepts, maxims, terse aphorisms or short exhortations."*[3] Other sayings are *benedictions* and *maledictions.*[4] Others are *parables*, such as we find in the Synoptic Gospels.[5] Still others are Jesus's *replies* to those posing questions.[6] Finally, as Edgar Hennecke writes:

> [I]t is convenient to make among the logia here collected a less formal distinction. Many are more or less identical with, or related to, sayings in the canonical Gospels. Nevertheless, with very few exceptions, even

---

[3] See Hennecke, *New Testament Apocrypha, Volume One: Gospels and Related Writings* (Philadelphia, 1963), 288 ff. Examples of these are logia 25, 41, 42, 56, 67, 80, 90, 92.
[4] Examples are logia 49, 58, 69, 87, 102, 112.
[5] Examples are 97 and 98.
[6] Examples are 12, 13, 18, 21, 43, 53, 60, 61, 72, 79, 114.

those which are most closely related to the canonical
logia do not reproduce them literally; they show variations of detail, or are formulated in a very different
way, and sometimes the situation too is altered. Some
are more developed than the corresponding Synoptic
sayings or parables [see logia 47, 64,].... In contrast
to these examples, other sayings are shorter and more
concise than their Synoptic parallels [see logion 63]....
In other cases, diverse Synoptic elements appear to
have been combined together. A curious example is
provided by Logion 16...of which the second half,
apart from an expansion at the end, is an obvious
abbreviation of Lk. 12:52 f., *so much so indeed that it
is scarcely comprehensible without reference to the Lucan
passage*...[emphasis added]

Rather than *Thomas* being a very early alternative source
for Jesus's original sayings, then, the evidence suggests
that the author(s)/editor(s) *already knew* the Synoptic tradition and adapted sayings taken from it. Since Hennecke
cites logion 16 in the quote directly above, we may note
one significant feature of it, which is repeated throughout the text: the use of the noun μοναχός ("*monachos*" =
"solitary one"/"monk"):

Jesus said, "Possibly people think that I have come to
cast peace on the world (cf. Matt. 10:34 and Lk. 12:
51), and they do not know that I have come to cast
divisions upon the earth (Lk. 12:51): fire (Lk. 12:49),
sword (Matt. 10:34), and war. For there shall be five
in a house: three shall be against two and two against
three, father against son, and son against father (see
Lk. 12:52 f.), and they shall stand as *solitary ones*."

Milan Vukomanović, in a fascinating article on *Thomas*'s use of the word *monachos*,[7] makes the case that *The*

---

[7] Prof. Milan Vukomanović, Ph.D (The University of Belgrade,
Faculty of Philosophy), "The Gospel of Thomas and Early Christian Monasticism in Egypt" (*Teologicka reflexe* 28; 2022), 3–25.
Vukomanović's article can be read online here: https://web.etf.
cuni.cz/ETFN-194-version1-tref_2022_1_sep_vukomanovic.pdf.

Gospel of Thomas evolved within early Egyptian ascetic (i.e., *monastic*) communities. Noting that the emergence of Christian asceticism in Egypt was a gradual process, incorporating within its burgeoning ascetic philosophy both Jewish "Wisdom" and Platonist elements from the Alexandrian context (remember, for instance, the Jewish Philo of Alexandria in the first century and the Christian Clement of Alexandria in the second), and finding its climax in the fourth century among desert ascetics, he sees the text of *Thomas* as evolving within that tradition. "One course of this inquiry into the Egyptian trajectory of *Thomas*," Vukomanović writes, "could perhaps lead from the earliest stages of consolidation of Jewish Christianity in Egypt, to the monastic asceticism of the desert fathers as the culminating point of such a development." In his view (which I find persuasive), the "Pachomian type of monastic community (named for St. Pachomius, the 'father' of cenobitic monasticism in Egypt)...could have composed the Coptic version (translation) of *GTh*. Indeed, several scholars have already associated this community with the compilation of the Nag Hammadi codices." Vukomanović concludes that, in its original form, "the *GTh* reached Alexandria from Palestine or Asia Minor, where it had already been in circulation in the first half of the second century." Subsequently, it was modified to suit the Egyptian ascetic context. One of those modifications appears to have been the insertion or elaboration of the ideal of the solitary ascetic (the "monk") into the text. Tellingly, *we have no texts earlier than Thomas* that employ the word *monachos* as a noun. In other words, Coptic *Thomas* is a text designed to be read by *monks*.

This brings us back to the differences that exist between the earlier Greek fragments and the Coptic version. René Falkenberg, in another illuminating article, compares logion 4 in Greek with the Coptic translation:

The Greek version reads: "[Jesus said,] 'A m[an old in day]s will not hesitate to ask a ch[ild seven day]s old about his place in [life and] he will [live.] For many of the f[irst] will be [last and] many of the last will be first and [...].'"

The Coptic version reads: "Jesus said, 'The man old in days will not hesitate to ask a small child seven days old about the place of life, and he will live. For many who are first will become last, and they will become solitary ones.'"[8]

Falkenberg, after presenting evidence of the logion's relatedness to sayings preserved in the canonical Gospels, shows how such a text would have resonated in the Pachomian monastic context, in which certain forms of behavior exemplified the monastic ideal ("they will become *solitary ones*" could simply mean "they will be *authentic monks*" — the sort of phrase one finds repeated, for instance, by Evagrius of Pontus in his ascetic writings). Falkenberg writes:

> Interestingly, such emphases in the Coptic fit a monastic context well, since monastic readers would recognize such wording from their everyday life. The senior person ("the old/elder [пɛⲗⲗⲟ, '*P-hllō*']") is the title of an experienced monk (or even a monastic leader), and the junior person ("a little, young child") could refer to a monk in training, not necessarily a young person but a newcomer to the monastic group, as Melissa H. Sellew has pointed out when comparing *Thomas* with the *Apophthegmata Patrum*. In monastic literature, an "elder" is far more honourable than an untrained "young" person. Yet, we have an intriguing example of the opposite in the *Bohairic Life of Pachomius*, where Pachomius asks his future successor, Theodore, to attend the instruction of his fellow monks:

---

[8] Hugo Lundhaug and Christian H. Bull (Editors), *The Nag Hammadi Codices as Monastic Books* (Tübingen, Germany, 2023), 87 ff. Falkenberg's full essay can be downloaded and read in full here: https://www.academia.edu/49567245/The_Single_Ones_in_the_Gospel_of_Thomas_A_Monastic_Perspective.

"When he came to [our father] who stood (ⲟⲍⲓ ⲉⲣⲁⲧϥ) speaking God's word to the brothers, Pachomius immediately took him by the hand in the midst of the brothers and said to him, 'Stand (ⲟⲍⲓ ⲉⲣⲁⲧⲕ) here and speak the holy words of God.' Although unwillingly, he began to speak in front of all the brothers who stood (ⲟⲍⲓ ⲉⲣⲁⲧⲟⲩ), including our father Pachomius who listened too like the brothers. Immediately some among them, out of pride, were angry and returned to their houses without listening to the Lord's word. They said, 'He is young (ⲕⲟⲩⲝⲓ) in age, but it is us who are elders (ⲃⲉⲗⲗⲟ), and it is to him that he gives order to instruct us!' In fact, Theodore was 33 the day our father made him stand (ⲧⲁⲍⲟϥ ⲉⲣⲁⲧϥ) to give the instruction, knowing that he was farther advanced than they."

This passage replays quite closely the scenario of logion 4 with the two persons of either "old (ⲍⲗ̄ⲗⲟ)" or "little/young (ⲕⲟⲩⲉⲓ)" age. In the *Bohairic Life*, the "elders (Bo. ⲃⲉⲗⲗⲟ = Sa. ⲍⲗ̄ⲗⲟ)" are also in need of instruction from the "young (Bo. ⲕⲟⲩⲝⲓ = Sa. ⲕⲟⲩⲉⲓ)" Theodore. Even if he here is 33 years old, he clearly is a junior compared to the more senior monks but nevertheless "farther advanced than they." Just after this passage, Pachomius scolds the angry elders for not paying attention to Theodore, and even quotes the New Testament saying, "Anyone, who may receive a little one (ⲟⲩⲁⲗⲟⲩ, Gr. παιδίον) in my name, receives me" (Matt 18:5). If we read logion 4 in such a monastic setting, the present passage of the *Bohairic Life* may also indicate whom the final sentence of logion 4 refers to when saying, "and *they* will be single ones," since both the old and the young would be "single ones (ⲟⲩⲁ ⲟⲩⲱⲧ)" in such a context.

As noted above, "and *they* will be single ones" could mean, quite plausibly, "and they will be true monks." Falkenberg continues by analyzing logion 30 in the two versions. Here are the texts:

Greek: [Jesus says, "Wh]ere they are [three (persons), they are] godless, but where o[ne] is alone, I say I am with him; raise the stone, there you will find me, split the wood, there I am."[9]

Coptic: Jesus said, "Where there are three gods, they are gods; where there are two or one, I am with him."

First, Falkenberg notes, "the two texts differ not only in wording and length but also in meaning, *where scholars find coherence in the Greek but consider the Coptic almost incomprehensible*" (emphasis added; this should remind us that the Coptic version—the allegedly "complete" version—cannot be relied upon to be either an accurate translation or as presenting unalloyed sayings of Jesus). He notes, second, that the Greek version appears to depend on Matthew 18:20. Falkenburg writes:

Our first concern is the Greek, which in the main seems dependent on the saying in Matthew, "Where two or three (τρεῖς) gather together in my name, there I am (ἐκεῖ εἰμι) among you" (18:20). Matthew presents here an early cultic service setting with the promise that Christ will be present when a minimum of two persons meet in his name. Since the Greek *Thomas* prefers one instead of more persons, only one person is promised closeness to Christ ("I am with him...you will find me"); such an intimacy is not possible for a group of people ("[three...are] godless")...

[W]e can confirm that the Greek makes more sense than the later Coptic translation. In his study on logion 30, Harold W. Attridge sums up the main findings in the text:

"Instead of an absolutely cryptic remark about gods being gods [in the Coptic], the fragment [in Greek] asserts that any *group* of people lacks divine presence. That presence is available only to the 'solitary one.' The importance of the solitary (μοναχός) is obvious in the

---

[9] The latter part of this logion appears in the Coptic version in logion 77b.

Gospel. Cf. sayings 11, 16, 22, 23, 49, 75 and 106. This saying must now be read in connection with those remarks on the 'monachos.'"[10]

In other words, the Coptic version of *The Gospel of Thomas* is probably not commenting, however obliquely, on the doctrine of the Trinity when it mentions "three gods" (as some have posited). Rather, it appears simply to be an unintelligible rendering — at least, it is unintelligible to us — of the Greek original. The original was championing — over against the collective — the ascetic ideal of the solitary one, to whom "the living Jesus" will reveal himself. One is reminded of the words of the desert father, Abba Alois: "Unless a man says in his heart, 'Only I and God are in the world,' he shall not find rest."[11]

Finally, this monastic ideal picks up on an early Christian ascetical understanding of sexuality and gender, the goal of which was to transcend biological distinctions. We see the seeds of such an ideal in Luke's version of an exchange between Jesus and the Sadducees. There Jesus says, "The sons of this age marry and are given in marriage, but *those accounted worthy* of sharing in that Age and in the resurrection of the dead *neither marry nor are given in marriage* [note the wording here — it could be taken as an inducement to embrace celibacy, something that is explicit in Matt. 19:11–12], for they cannot even die any more, for they are the *equals of angels*, for they are *God's sons*, being *sons of the resurrection*" (Luke 20:34–36; emphasis added; compare Matt. 22:23 ff.; Mark 12:18 ff.).[12] Relatedly, one might compare Paul's words in Galatians 3:28, his exhortation to celibacy in 1 Corinthians 7:1, 6–8, and the 144,000 *male* virgins in Revelation 7:3–8 and 14:1 — indeed, what was to become the "monastic" ideal appears quite early.

---

[10] Ibid.

[11] Cf. Owen Chadwick, editor, *Western Asceticism* (Philadelphia, 1957), 132. *Apophthegmata Patrum*, XI, 5.

[12] D. B. Hart, *The New Testament*, 2nd ed. (Yale, 2023).

Considering the passage from Luke above, I believe it is highly probable that when *The Gospel of Thomas* speaks of "*knowing oneself*," it is picking up on this very theme. It means, in other words, "knowing oneself *to be a son of God*": "When you *know yourselves*, then shall you be known, and yo*u shall know that you are the sons of the living Father*. But if ye do not know yourselves, then you are in poverty, and you are poverty" (logion 3; emphasis added). "The sons of God" are those who, being "solitary ones," have transcended gender (and other) differences; they are "like the angels," "sons of the resurrection" (meaning, they are no longer defined by biological standards). So it is that logion 22 reads:

> Jesus said to them, "When (2OTⲀN) you make the two one, and when you make the inside like the outside, and the outside like the inside, and the above like the below, and you shall do that in order to make the male and the female into this *single one* (ϕⲟ‸ⲟⲩⲧ ⲙ̄ⲛ̄ ⲧⲥ2ⲓⲙⲉ ⲙ̄ⲡⲟⲩⲁ ⲟⲩⲱⲧ), so that the male will not be male and the female not female, when (2OTⲀN) you make eyes instead of eye, hand instead of hand, foot instead of foot, image (2ⲓⲕⲱⲛ‸) instead of image, then (ⲧⲟⲧⲉ) you shall enter [the king]dom."

The kernel of this saying — "the two will be(come) one . . . the male and the female . . . etc." — appears to be an authentic saying of Jesus, found in other early Christian texts. It is quoted in the mid-second-century text known as *II Clement* (12:2): "For when the Lord himself was asked by someone when his kingdom would come, he said, 'When the two shall be one, and the outside as the inside, and the male with the female neither male nor female.'" (The author goes on, in 12:5, to interpret the saying: "And by 'the male with the female neither male nor female' he means this, that when a brother sees a sister he should have no thought of her as female, nor she of him as male.")[13]

---

[13] *Apostolic Fathers I*, Loeb Classical Library (Cambridge MA/ London, 1985), 147, 149.

Similarly, Clement of Alexandria, in his *Stromata* (iii, 13), presents the same saying, citing *The Gospel of the Egyptians* (note that both Clement and the apocryphal Gospel he quotes are *Egyptian* in provenance, just as both the Greek and Coptic versions of *Thomas* are). Again, what we discern in this saying of Jesus are the roots of what would grow into the ideal of the monk.

And this same idea informs what is for many the most unappealing of the logia in *Thomas*—it is the final logion in the book, in fact: logion 114:

> Simon Peter said to them: Let Mary go forth from among us, for women are not worthy of the life. Jesus said: Behold, I shall lead her, that I may make her male, in order that she also may become a living spirit like you males. For every woman who makes herself male shall enter into the kingdom of heaven.

Given that the Jesus of the canonical Gospels never suggests that women are deficient or must become "male," it seems likely that *Thomas* 114 is an adulterated logion attributed to Jesus. However, its intention (especially in light of logion 22) appears to be something other than merely misogynistic; the implication is that—ascetically—a true ascetic can transcend sexual distinctions. Indeed, in the desert tradition of Egypt and Palestine, we have instances of female monastics who intentionally made themselves masculine in appearance and behavior. We find in *Thomas* 114, perhaps, both the echo of a spiritual ideal espoused by Jesus and the beginnings of a distortion of that ideal.

To conclude, what one makes of *The Gospel of Thomas* depends on how one approaches it. If one wishes to find in it a "Jesus" more authentic, more "inclusive," more "spiritual"—and so on—than the multifaceted Jesus of the four canonical Gospels, one will need to interpret it quite creatively to keep from becoming disillusioned with it over time. *Thomas* presents us with no positive alternative to the Jesus of the church's canon, no matter how intriguing or stimulating many of its logia are. The four NT Gospels became canonical (the word "canon" means something by which we measure other things) for good reason: they were the ones the vast majority of Christians treasured most and regarded as genuinely representing Jesus as they experienced him. They constituted the original apostolic deposit, *the authentic tradition* as written. Jesus as he's presented in *Thomas*, in comparison, is an elusive figure, hard in temperament, rigorous, and one might even say spiritually elitist, whose appeal seems to have been limited to a relative minority of Egyptian ascetics. While one can appreciate some of the logia of *The Gospel of Thomas*, one will find in them nothing of the mercy, forgiveness, charity, healing, encouragement, or the message of resurrection that suffuses the four Gospels.

APPENDIX 2
A Quick Walk Through the Canon

1.

Traditionally, Christians do not read the Bible simply as "a book." Rather, they recognize it to be a *collection*, a *library* of books. And when scripture is referred to as "the word of God," what is meant is that, in the books of the Bible, we find a collective, evolving testimony. God, of course, is its central concern, and those who wrote the books it comprises over a span of centuries were divinely "inspired" (or "influenced"). It is a misconception to imagine that the Bible speaks with one voice. It doesn't contain only one perspective, it isn't monolithic, and it isn't without the contradictions and shortcomings endemic to human agency (to quote Emerson, "A foolish consistency is the hobgoblin of little minds"), or even "debates" (for lack of a better word) between viewpoints expressed among its various texts (a feature about which both the great rabbis and the church fathers were aware). Traditionally, when Christians say it is "inspired"—that is, "God-breathed" (2 Tim. 3:16; θεόπνευστος, "*theopneustos*")—they don't mean that it was dictated word-for-word—that may be claimed by Muslims for the Quran, but it isn't a Christian belief where the Bible is concerned. A memorable line in 2 Peter puts the Christian view succinctly: "Men moved by [or, 'carried along by'] the Holy Spirit ['Breath'] spoke from God" (1:21). To say that scripture is "God-breathed" means that writers were swept up and borne along by a compelling insight, one bestowed on them by God, which they then expressed in words according to their best abilities and understanding. Taken as a whole, then, the biblical canon is a united but diverse testimony; for Christians, that testimony is brought to its fullness and given its interpretive "key" with Jesus Christ and his message of the kingdom of God. Christ himself is the culminating revelation — "the Word of God" made flesh — who sheds light on both the adequacies and inadequacies of all that came before him, recorded in the scriptural record.

One way to describe "biblical fundamentalism," as contrasted with the traditional Christian understanding of the Bible, is to say that what the former does, in effect, is *flatten* all the biblical books, putting them all on the same even level. It makes the rough places plain, certainly — unfortunately, however, plain in the sense that a checkerboard is. What happens in the flattening process is that the "mountains" and "valleys" of the Bible disappear entirely, and we are left with the wholly mistaken view that the Bible is a single book, written by a single author (God), in which every passage is to be received as of equal value with every other passage (an unsustainable view if one reads the texts thoroughly), and the whole tome is interpreted *literally* (also unsustainable for any serious and intelligent reader). In other words, a strict fundamentalist reading of the Bible would require one to regard a passage in Leviticus (let's say one that gives instructions about the high priest's undergarments) as of equal value with the Beatitudes.

By any standard, of course, the Bible can be a confusing mixture of genres: fable, legend, history, parables, sayings, prophecies, letters, hymns, and so forth. Shockingly (for some), it includes irreverence, including some cynicism (Job, Ecclesiastes), humor (Jonah), and even erotic poetry (the Song of Songs). The Bible, as we've said, is a collection of many books, written and edited over centuries. The Christian "canon" is made up of two canons, that of the Old Covenant (the Hebrew Bible) and that of the New. The word "canon" literally means "measuring reed," a standard of measurement like a yardstick. In this instance, the *canon* of scripture provides the dimensions and limits of the revelation as contained in the apostolic, catholic, orthodox Tradition (what has been called "the life of the Holy Spirit in the Church"), so that those who carry on its legacy into their own times might do so faithfully. The Bible doesn't comprise the entirety of the revelation or the Tradition. Taken together, the Old and New Testament canons provide the essential conceptual context for understanding Jesus's message. For Christian believers, then, Jesus is the key to unlocking the meaning of the scriptures overall, and the scriptures—in all their variety and occasional contrariness—lead readers to a more accurate interpretation of his teachings (Luke 24:27, 45).

2.

To see more clearly how we read the canon, it helps to look at its "shape"—its "table of contents," in other words. Neither the Old Testament (whether in its somewhat differing Orthodox, Catholic, or Protestant version) nor the New Testament is merely a slapdash, thrown-together collection of texts. There is a reason that the shape of each canon taken separately, and that of both canons looked at side by side, are arranged as they are. Quite noticeably, the organization to be seen in each canon *is paralleled* by that of the other. That is to say that the two tables of contents placed side by side tell us something important about the overall structure of the Christian Bible. Viewed as a *diptych*, the twofold canon presents us with an integrated single message.

To understand that message, we might begin by asking a series of questions: *Why these books, and not others that could have been included? Why do some of them seem to contradict or "debate with" other books in the canon? What is the relationship between the Testaments, and how does the New affect our reading of the Old? Why are the books ordered as they are, and does the order itself mean anything?* And so on.

Two aspects of the canon in particular are important to consider. These are:

First, the Bible reflects an evolutionary process.

Second, the shape of the canon is directly related to the self-understanding of the church — it is a matter of communal identity and continuity.

I will look at these aspects one at a time, and then suggest how an understanding of them can aid an intelligent and reverent interpretation of it. I intend to keep these remarks as uncomplicated and basic as possible, wishing merely to present here a few general notes about the character of the canon as Christians receive it. Differences between versions of the canon (between the Hebrew Masoretic text and the Greek Septuagint, for instance, or between the Catholic, Orthodox, Protestant, and Ethiopian canons) will be left unaddressed, as will other details about the subject.

(1) The Bible reflects an evolutionary process

A "flat" fundamentalist reading of the Bible involves, among other things, a failure to recognize in it an evolution in the understanding of the God who reveals himself. The unfolding of biblical revelation is observable in the Old Testament (OT) in particular. We should bear in mind that the OT was composed and edited over the course of centuries, roughly spanning a thousand years (by comparison, the New Testament was composed over a space of only five decades at most). During that long stretch of time, there was a great development within Hebrew religion, frequently the result of its history and interaction with other cultures (Egyptian, Canaanite, Philistine, Babylonian, Assyrian, Persian, Greek, and — beginning in the age of the Maccabees — Roman). Israel's evolving understanding of God can be seen in what I call its internal "debates," which I mentioned above. To put the matter concisely, there is a maturation in the Hebrew depiction of God — from YHWH, perceived as a tribal deity, to his being perceived as the universal and only God, from an anthropomorphic deity (and even one who at times changes his mind—he "repents" at times of decisions he has made, e.g., Gen. 6:6; 1 Sam. 15:11) to his being understood as the supreme Lord of heaven and earth, and from "henotheism" (i.e., "our" God, although supreme and the chief of gods, is one god among others) to "monotheism" (there exists but one God, and there are no others).

There has always been a vigorous "debating" tradition among rabbis, especially over matters of Torah. Such debate has been a feature of the Jewish faith for millennia, and even debating with God is not off limits in Jewish piety. It's a mark of their living faith. It shouldn't surprise us, then, that the most sacred Jewish texts reveal a similar characteristic. The Bible is a book encompassing many generations and the works of numerous contributors, in which a lot of hashing out takes place in its texts. The OT, in other words, isn't a flat text. Jews hold the first five books, those "of Moses," to be "the Word of God" in a privileged sense that the rest of the OT doesn't share. The other canonical writings carry on the Word of God, but they don't carry the same weight of authority, nor are they esteemed as highly as the Pentateuch. (This, as we shall see, is mirrored in the NT with the special reverence accorded the four Gospels in classical Christianity.)

To take just two examples, one internal "debate" in the OT involves what I have called elsewhere "conventional piety." Since I have gone into some detail on that issue in my book, *Knowing Darkness*,[1] I won't belabor the point here. It's enough to mention that a hallmark of OT "conventional piety"—what can be seen in, for instance, the book of Proverbs (another classic expression is Psalm 37, or Ps. 36 in the LXX)—is the idea that God rewards righteous behavior and punishes evildoers during their lives.

---

[1] "Job and the Problem of Conventional Piety," chap. 5 in *Knowing Darkness: On Skepticism, Melancholy, Friendship, and God* (Eerdmans, 2009), 73 ff.

The problem, of course, is that it is frequently the case that the good suffer and the wicked prosper; later generations of wisdom writers dealt with those obvious facts of life head-on. The authors of Job and Ecclesiastes in particular mimicked texts of conventional piety found in earlier Wisdom writers, only to turn the tables and challenge directly the very grounds of such assumptions. Neither of these astringent books repudiated morality, righteousness, or the holiness of God, but they took the argument to a different and more sophisticated level. Overall, we have a debate of existential issues in the Wisdom books of the OT; and the fact that, alongside Psalms and Proverbs, we find that such countervailing and straightforwardly disturbing books as Job and Ecclesiastes also made the final cut, should signal us that the canon is not a uniform text with a single, flat moral and theological viewpoint.

Another example of an internal canonical "debate" in the OT regards the proper attitude the Jewish people should take toward gentiles—including their most despised enemies. To see this, one can contrast the harsh approach in Ezra 9 and 10 towards those who had married gentile wives after the Babylonian exile (with Ezra's insistence that the wives be sent packing), with the gentle book of Ruth (a late book in the canon), in which the heroine and great-grandmother of King David is revealed to have been a Moabite woman. Moabites, it should be recalled, were especially detested gentiles, even said to be the fruit of the abomination of incest (Gen. 19:37).

Similarly, one can contrast the sheer glee with which the prophet Nahum describes the historical destruction of Assyrian Nineveh in 612 BC, with the parabolic irony of the (fictional and humorously exaggerated) book of Jonah towards that same deeply hated gentile city many years later. There was certainly no love on Nahum's (or most Jews') part for the brutal Assyrians. The latter, after all, had destroyed the Northern Kingdom of Israel with extraordinary savagery in the 720s BC and had deported, in a cruel forced march, the survivors. The book of Jonah, for its part, is one of the latest books of the Hebrew canon, written three hundred years or more after the fall of the Northern Kingdom. It can, indeed, be said to be a parable. It asks the question, "*What if* the Assyrian Ninevites had repented?" It is a humorous work, with the only unpleasant person in the story being the disobedient prophet (a parody of those who, like Ezra many years before, had nothing but disdain for all gentiles). All around the prophet Jonah in the story, from the pagans onboard the ship who regretfully cast him into the deep (1:16), to the hateful Ninevites themselves (3:5–10), gentiles keep turning to God for mercy and he, in turn, shows them his kindness — much to the petulant and bloodthirsty prophet's chagrin. Jonah sulks and rebukes God angrily, because God proves merciful (4:2–3). This gem of a book ends with a baited hook of a question that's really intended to catch the reader. In essence, it asks, "Will *you* be merciful as God is merciful, or will *you* be bitter, bigoted, and angry like Jonah?" This not only is a question meant to prick the conscience of the audience but a rejection of the idea that God hates gentiles and desires their destruction. Even the most dreaded gentiles, like the Assyrians, stand a chance with God. So, as Ezra is countered by Ruth, so Nahum is countered by Jonah. The internal canonical debate hashes out what sort of God it is whom Israel worships, and, along with that concern, what sort of people those who worship him should be as a consequence.

Turning to Christian readers, the OT can only be viewed logically as a *progressive revelation*. It is progressing towards an ever-fuller revelation of God. "Truly, I say to you, many prophets and righteous men longed to see what you see, and did not see it, and to hear what you hear, and did not hear it" (Matt. 13:17). The import of the statements of Jesus in the Sermon on the Mount, in which he says, "You have heard that it was said ... but I say to you" (Matt. 5:21–22, 27–28, 31–32, 33–34, 38–39, 43–44),

should be appreciated for the claims to superior revelation
that they are. Jesus means that he is *correcting* all previous
misconceptions about God's ways. He sets himself up as
the definitive interpreter of Torah, the One who fulfills
("brings to fullness" or "completes") "the law and the
prophets" (Matt. 5:17). Without him, in other words, the
OT is inconclusive. He points his followers to the spirit
of righteousness, not to the letter of the Law. The Gospel
of John, going further along these lines, says of Jesus that
he is "the Word of God" who "became flesh," and that he
alone "has made [God] known" (John 1:1, 14, 18). The word
"known" in John 1:18 is *exegesato*—"exegeted." It is the
same word we use when we speak of *interpreting*—"reading out of" or "exegeting"—a text, be it a biblical or any
other written source. Like an otherwise indecipherable
text, God has been *interpreted* to us by Jesus, the enfleshed
"Word," both the perfect interpreter and interpretation.

The Christian, looking back over the OT, views it as a
vast landscape of highs and lows. It isn't a tableland, but
a terrain with various features—many that are exquisitely
beautiful and some ghastly. The OT is uneven, and it
depicts—like a series of pictures in a family photo album
taken over a long stretch of years—a slow progression
toward greater maturity. It isn't God himself who evolves
in the OT texts but rather the understanding of who God
is on the part of the people of Israel. The OT depicts an
evolution, then. It's only when one regards the Bible as
a flat text, with every jot considered equally important,
that contradictions are seen as a threat, and difficulties
for any reasonable appreciation of the Bible become
insurmountable.

For Christians, the Bible is "the Word of God" only
insofar as it leads toward Jesus Christ and the gospel,
consequently measured by the perfect standard they set.
Passages in the NT show that early Christians read the
OT in just that way. In 2 Corinthians 3, for instance, Paul
contrasts the two Testaments, his most telling statement

in the passage perhaps being this one: We apostles are, he says, "ministers of a new covenant, not in a written code [literally, 'word'] but in the Spirit; for the written code ['word'] kills, but the Spirit gives life" (vs. 6). The OT, he says, is written "with ink" and "on tablets of stone" (vs. 3); it is "a dispensation of death" (vs. 7) and "a dispensation of condemnation" (vs. 9), and it will "fade away" (vs. 11). These are tough words indeed. And, in contrast, the gospel of Christ is written "with the Spirit of the living God" and "on tablets of human [literally, 'fleshly'] hearts" (vs. 3); it is "a dispensation of the Spirit...with greater splendor" (vs. 8), and it is "permanent" (vs. 11). What's more, the Old Covenant cannot be unveiled and properly understood without recourse to the New Covenant in Christ (vss. 12–18). In Galatians, we find Paul again making a sustained argument in Chapters 3 and 4 along similar lines. The Law of Moses, he says straightforwardly, is inferior to the gospel. Paul allows that the Law leads to Christ (3:24), but—once he has come—it is subsumed and interpreted in the light of Christ's higher teaching. Paul makes the same point in Romans 10:4, where he writes, "For Christ is the end ['goal'] of the law." When he writes in Galatians 3:19 that the Law "was ordained by angels through an intermediary [i.e., Moses]," he is saying that the transmission of it had not come directly from God, but *indirectly*—passed through intermediate hands (angelic and human agency) before being received by Israel. The implication is that, though good, the Law isn't utterly reliable and certainly not perfect. Paul reads the OT with the critical mind of a first-century rabbi, like his contemporary Philo. He prefers a "spiritual" (allegorical) reading to a strictly literal reading of the text, thus avoiding the difficulties that a literalistic reading would present. Indeed, Paul never interprets the OT *without recourse to allegory*. All the NT writers, it can be said, assume that there was an evolution in the biblical revelation, which culminated in Christ.

This brings us to the New Testament.

*(2) The shape of the canon is directly related to the self-
understanding of the church*

Like the OT, the NT reflects the community that gave
it its shape. Unlike the OT, however, it is made up of
texts written over a period of, roughly speaking, fifty
years, the earliest (probably 1 Thessalonians) dating to
AD 52, and the latest to a decade or two before 100. However, although the NT *writings* are all first-century books,
the *canon* in its final "shape" reflects a settled fourth-
century church. More specifically still, we have inherited a
Roman (including both its Western and Eastern "halves")
"Petrine-Pauline" canon, and the twenty-seven books that
make it up are arranged to highlight that fact.

The writings in the NT include occasional letters (by or
attributed to Paul, James, Peter, John, and Jude), general
exhortations or sermons addressed to churches (Hebrews
and 1 John; possibly also James and 1 Peter), four Gospels,
a book of history (Acts), and a single, concluding work of
prophecy. Apart from these texts, we have no other Christian writings that can be dated with confidence to the first
century.[2] That the NT texts were collected and preserved
from a very early date is obvious, showing that they were
soon accounted sacred. Already, in the first century, Paul's
letters were being read in some churches as holy scripture — the Second Epistle of Peter says so explicitly: "So
also our beloved brother Paul wrote to you according to
the wisdom given him, speaking as he does in all his letters.
There are some things hard in them to understand, which
the ignorant and unstable twist to their own destruction,
as they do the other scriptures" (3:15–16; emphasis mine).
From the earliest decades of the church's existence, then,
a canon was in the process of being formed. Likewise, as
this snippet from 2 Peter reveals, there were evidently
"right" and "wrong" ways one could read the same texts.
In short, "orthodoxy" was an issue from the outset.

---

[2] Although it is possible that, among the writings of the apostolic
fathers, the *Didache* might be dated that early.

In addition to the "ignorant and unstable twisting" of apostolic writings, hundreds of other writings were produced during the second and third centuries, many of them bearing the names of first-century apostles. Some of these later works would be deemed orthodox and even canonical in various churches, some would be read devotionally but never treated seriously as canon. Still others represent alternative "canons" (for lack of a more precise phrase) in heterodox churches. One of the chief purposes of having an "orthodox" canon of writings, it must be noted, was precisely to distinguish between orthodoxy and heterodoxy, truth and falsehood, and authenticity and non-authenticity. The content of the NT, as it took shape, was based on whether the texts in question came from Christian *antiquity* (i.e., datable to the first century), and considered *apostolic* in origin, or at least written by someone close to an apostle (thus, for instance, Mark on behalf of Peter, Luke on behalf of Paul). Also, of importance was whether a particular text was *read widely* as scripture throughout the churches and adhered to — or, at least, didn't contradict — the generally accepted orthodox *regula fidei* (one can find one early example of this in what we know as "The Apostles' Creed"). *Antiquity*, *apostolicity*, *catholicity*, and *orthodoxy* were thus the four marks of those texts considered worthy of inclusion in the church's canon. Tradition, in other words, preceded canon.

The period 140–200 was decisive for the canon as we now have it, as early Christian writers such as Justin Martyr, Irenaeus of Lyons, Clement of Alexandria, Tertullian, and others give evidence. To counter the heresies of the period, churches in the Roman world felt compelled to draw up lists of canons for use in their worship. These lists of approved books overlapped for the most part, with some canons having more books in them and some having less, some including books that our familiar NT does not include, and some excluding books that ours contains. Canons could vary from locale to locale, a fact which suggests a more flexible attitude in these centuries towards biblical inspiration than would be the case in the century following. If the other guiding norms of the *regula fidei* and apostolically ordained oversight were in place, it seems a more open-ended outlook was possible between regional churches.

The fourth century, of course, altered things in a way that continues to the present day. With the arrival of Constantine and his heirs had come the hope that there could be a uniform creedal orthodoxy, a unified episcopate, and one Bible used throughout the empire (that was their wish, at any rate, even though the reality was never quite so tidy as that). It was during the latter half of this momentous age that the canon of the NT as we have it today became fixed.

No council of the church decided it officially at the time (surprisingly, that was to occur for the very first time at the Council of Trent of the Roman Catholic Church in the sixteenth century). The first list we have that contains the twenty-seven books of our NT comes from Athanasius, the Patriarch of Alexandria. It was the custom for that Patriarch to write an encyclical to the churches under his oversight each year in preparation for the Easter celebration. In his thirty-ninth such letter for the year 367, he lists the canonical books of both testaments, though the NT books are (significantly) not given in the same order as we have them in our Bibles. For example, the letters of James, Peter, John, and Jude immediately follow Acts, and then come the Pauline epistles. These books only, Athanasius writes, "are the fountains of salvation," and no one is "to add to these... [or] take ought from these." He lists, as well, other writings that the fathers recommend as useful and instructive, but he sternly warns against heretical writings that "beguile" and "lead astray." In short, this list is poised against heretical writings on the one hand, and as a reliable standard by which to measure the worth of other orthodox writings on the other.[3]

When Athanasius composed this letter, his "see" (or "seat" — a term indicating a bishop's throne, and thus his authority) in Alexandria was one of the three great "Petrine" sees of the empire. The other two were Rome and Antioch in Syria, with Rome taking the primacy among them. These three sees claimed, one way or another, a vital association with the apostle Peter, upon whose person and extraordinary conviction, it was believed, the church had been built (Matt. 16:17–19). To these three apostolic sees was later added in importance that of Constantinople, and finally the status of the original mother church, Jerusalem, was restored.

For the early church, with the loss of Jerusalem's oversight after AD 71, Peter became the recognized symbol and touchstone of apostolic tradition. It was around the central figure of Peter that other apostolic figures and their writings (Paul and John, for example) were gathered and, in a sense, found their legitimacy. This was a development in the Roman church's self-understanding (by "Roman," I include all those domains that came under Roman sway). Let me be clear at this point, I am not referring to the papacy. There was no "papacy" as it exists today during the early centuries of the church. There was a primacy accorded to the church in Rome, not simply because Rome was the imperial seat (although, of course, that was hardly a negligible factor), but because it was there that the most important apostles, Peter and Paul, had met their deaths. The "Roman" church was multifaceted in the first century, under numerous "overseers" and "elders" ("bishops" and/or "priests"), and — in the city itself — made up of various congregations and, it seems, various

---

[3] Philip Schaff, D.D., L.L.D. and Henry Wace, D.D., *A Select Library of the Christian Church: Nicene and Post-Nicene Fathers (Second Series), Volume 4: Athanasius: Select Works and Letters* (Hendrickson Publishers, 1999), 551–52.

congregational "styles." The foundation of genuineness and the source of unity between them was their share in the heritage of Peter and Paul, with Peter's status being the more significant due to his close companionship with Jesus during his earthly ministry. This would, in time, be applied to the development of the Roman see, and — with the loss of the other great Petrine sees to Islam, and with the "great schism" between Rome and Constantinople in 1054 — Rome would emerge as the sole Petrine see in the West and the papacy would come into its own. But it is only the threefold fourth-century emphasis on *Peter*, *Paul*, and *Rome* with which we are concerned here. It is those three first-century "markers" that contributed significantly to the shape that the NT canon would assume finally and permanently for all Christians.

It was the Latin Vulgate that settled the ordering of the NT's table of contents for Bibles ever since. Commissioned by Pope Damasus I in 382, and largely the work of the brilliant, notoriously irascible, and mercurial St Jerome, it became the standard Latin translation of the Bible. The NT books were the same as those listed in Athanasius's Festal Letter of 367, reflecting the same agreed-upon canon of the church, but it reordered the books so that the Letters of Paul preceded the book of Acts and the other epistles (much later, the book of Acts would come between the Gospels and Paul's Letters). The Epistle to the Romans conspicuously now headed the list of collected apostolic letters. The Vulgate's table of contents visibly — and thus significantly — put "Rome" at the forefront. Likewise, the OT canon was reordered. Instead of its tripartite Hebrew division (the five books of Moses, followed by the Prophets, and then the "writings"), the Christian OT was divided into *four* sections: the *five books of Moses*, the *historical books*, the *books of poetry and Wisdom*, and *the Prophets*. The outliers, appended to the end of the OT's contents, were I and II Maccabees. The NT canon roughly corresponds to these categories, with a similar *fourfold* division into *four Gospels*

(= five books of Moses), one *historical book* (Acts, which in the original Vulgate ordering was inserted between Hebrews and James), the *"wisdom" of the apostles' epistles*, and one *book of prophecy* (Revelation). The NT is thus presented as the continuation and complement of the OT, the two lists of contents visibly "mirroring" one another, becoming as it were a sort of diptych.

To take these observations a step further, to understand the NT canon in its final, fourth-century, Roman "shape," we can tick off the following points: *First*, it *establishes accommodating doctrinal boundaries*. *Second*, it *identifies* the *church* as that founded by Christ. *Third*, it *traces* the church's historical shift, geographically and influentially, from its original center in *Jerusalem* to the imperial center, *Rome*, from whence it continued to spread *to the end of the earth* (cf. Acts 1:8). *Fourth*, it *stresses* the roles in that movement played by Rome's two preeminent apostles, *Peter and Paul*. We will take these one at a time.

"First, it *establishes accommodating doctrinal boundaries"*: The NT groups together a generously wide range of first-century texts. We have become so accustomed to the elements that bind the collection together as a whole that we sometimes fail to notice the differences between the various texts. The Christology of Mark is not identical to that of John's Gospel (although they're not as different as we might at first suppose — Mark certainly identifies Jesus as divine), for instance, and neither is it to the Letter to the Hebrews. This is not to say, obviously, that they are in conflict, *but that they are bound together as distinctive aspects of a single Tradition*. The boundaries of orthodoxy, then, were not so rigidly narrow that they could not embrace the assortment of views found in Mark and John, Luke and Revelation, Paul and James.

"Second, it *identifies* the *Church* as that founded by Christ"*: This is established in the very first Gospel in the canon, and it is the reason why Matthew was both recognized from the very beginning as "the ecclesiastical

Gospel" and likewise why—as the canon developed under
the auspices of the "Petrine" sees—it was placed prom-
inently at the head of the canon. What is the Church?
Who are these people who proclaim that Jesus is Lord and
Christ? The answer to these questions about the Christian
community's identity begins to take shape in the very first
text in the canon to use the word "church," which is Matthew's Gospel: "And I tell you, you are Peter, and on this
rock I will build my church..." (Matt. 16:18). The Church,
then, is that community that Jesus established with Peter.
And Peter's churches (Rome, Antioch, and Alexandria—
the latter said to be "Petrine" because, as traditionally
claimed, it had been established through Peter's "interpreter," Mark) were first among the churches, just as
Peter himself had stood as the "first" (*protos*) among the
Twelve to whom Jesus had given apostolic authority (Matt.
10:1–4). Peter's primacy is a given in Matthew, and the
church's identity as the original Church, built by Christ,
cannot be dissociated from him as its foundation.

And this brings us to the third and fourth points concerning the canon that I wish to mention, which we must
take together. So—

"*Third*, it *traces* the church's historical shift, geographically and influentially, from its original center in *Jerusalem*
to the imperial center, *Rome*, from whence it continued
to spread *to the end of the earth* (cf. Acts 1:8)"; and "*Fourth*,
it *stresses* the roles in that movement played by Rome's
two preeminent apostles, *Peter and Paul.*" With these two
statements in mind, then, here is a quick overview of the
shape of the NT as it comes to us filtered through the
three Petrine sees of Rome, Antioch, and Alexandria,
and finally, through the papal Roman see, as reflected
in the Vulgate's list of NT texts:

1. *The Four Gospels—Matthew, Mark, Luke, and John.*

As we noted above, Matthew takes the lead. Composed,
it seems likely, in Antioch, it is the Gospel most concerned
to clarify the church's identity, with Peter as the rallying

point and foundation stone, his apostolic status being that of the "first" among equals. This would have legitimated, in the minds of early Christians, the roles of the sees of Antioch, Rome, and Alexandria, which derived their authority from Peter, either directly or (as in the case of Alexandria) through one of his closest disciples (i.e., Mark).

Matthew, then, having based the church's identity on the person and message of Peter, is followed by "the Gospel of Peter" himself—because, as the earliest Fathers (Irenaeus, for example) tell us, *Mark* merely put down in writing what *Peter* had proclaimed.

Alongside Peter stands Paul in the early Roman Christian mind, the other apostle who was martyred in the Eternal City; and so Luke, the third Gospel, is "the Gospel of Paul," for Luke was that apostle's great companion. The Gospel of Luke is only one half of a two-part work, with the book of Acts being the second half (together, Luke and Acts are sometimes called the *Iliad* and the *Odyssey* of the NT); but the canon divides these two halves.

The Gospel of John has the highest Christology in the NT and is considered "the spiritual Gospel" by the early church. It crowns the other three. But it *concludes*—as Matthew's began, so to speak—*by establishing Peter and his authority*, along with a prophecy concerning his death, which every reader would have known had occurred in Rome: "Feed my sheep [i.e., be the Shepherd of my people]. Truly, truly, I say to you, when you were young, you girded yourself and walked where you would; but when you are old, you will stretch out your hands, and another will gird you and carry you where you do not wish to go...Follow me" (John 21:17–19).

So, the Four Gospels, in addition to recording the acts and words of Jesus, also identify the church as that founded upon *Peter*, whose gospel—along with that of *Paul*, his spiritual if not his actual companion in ministry—is the true, apostolic one, whose words continue to feed the sheep of Christ.

2. *The Epistles of Paul: Romans, 1 and 2 Corinthians, Galatians, Ephesians, Philippians, Colossians, 1 and 2 Thessalonians,
1 and 2 Timothy, Titus, Philemon, Hebrews.* Before proceed-
ing further, it's necessary to say beforehand that the "Pauline corpus" is made up of books that are genuinely by
Paul and some that are in dispute as to their authenticity.
Romans, the two letters to the Corinthians, Galatians,
Philippians, 1 Thessalonians, and Philemon are indisput-
ably by Paul. Ephesians, Colossians, and 2 Thessalonians
are disputed. That said, I fully accept their authenticity.
The Pastoral Epistles (1 and 2 Timothy and Titus) are
considered by most modern scholars as being not by Paul,
although — again — I accept them as authentic (both the
renowned British scholar J. N. D. Kelly, who wrote a fine
commentary on the Pastoral Epistles, and Luke Timothy Johnson, have argued for the plausibility of Pauline
authorship, and I find their views persuasive[4]). Hebrews
was only accorded Pauline authorship with some ambiv-
alence from the earliest period (the mention of Paul's
companion, Timothy, in 13:23 certainly encouraged the
notion of Pauline authorship, but it might just as easily
indicate that another from among Paul's circle — for
example, Silas — might have written it).[5]

In this light, we notice that — unlike other arrange-
ments of the NT canon — the Vulgate puts Romans at the
head, right after Acts. By putting the texts in this order,

[4] See J. N. D. Kelly, *The Pastoral Epistles* (London: A & C Black,
1963); and Luke Timothy Johnson, *The First and Second Letters
to Timothy: A New Translation with Introduction and Commentary*,
Anchor Bible (Yale, 2001).
[5] Many books of worth come to mind for an introductory study
of Paul. In my opinion, Douglas A. Campbell's books on Paul,
beginning with *Paul: An Apostle's Journey* (Eerdmans, 2018), stand
among the best in contemporary Pauline studies. For a collection
of translated primary texts and valuable essays, it is hard to top
The Writings of St. Paul: A Norton Critical Edition, 2nd ed., edited by
Wayne A. Meeks and John T. Fitzgerald (W. W. Norton & Co.,
2007). Another useful little book is *Paul: A Very Short Introduction*,
by E. P. Sanders (Oxford University Press, 2001).

in the canon's final arrangement, *we have Paul preaching the gospel in Rome at the end of Acts, immediately followed by the epistle in which he fleshes out his message as addressed to that same city.*

In geographical terms, the Pauline corpus moves from Rome and the West eastwards, concluding on the outskirts, if you will, of Jerusalem with the Epistle (or, perhaps it might better be called the Homily) to the Hebrews. We might note the clear implication that the center of authoritative gravity has shifted west from Jerusalem in this salutation: "Those who come from Italy send you greetings" (Heb. 13:24).

Hebrews ends on a rather poignant note, with the exhortation to "remember your leaders [who are deceased], those who spoke to you the word of God; consider the outcome of their life and imitate their faith" (13:7). Hebrews 13:9 ("it is well that the heart be strengthened by grace, not by foods, which have not benefited their adherents"—a reference to matters of "foods" in Jewish law) even echoes faintly Paul's words in Romans 14:17 ("For the kingdom of God is not meat and drink"—again, referring to Jewish regulations concerning food), thus bringing such tense early Jewish Christian concerns full circle. It goes on to issue a call that Hebrew Christians leave behind the synagogues that have repudiated them ("We have an altar from which those who serve the tent have no right to eat [I see in this a clear reference to the Eucharist] .... Therefore let us go forth to him outside the camp and bear the abuse he endured"; 13:10–14).

3. *The book of the Acts of the Apostles.* Acts continues the story begun in the Gospel of Luke. Although it tells of the Twelve, including the replacement of Judas the traitor with Matthias, and the leadership of James, "the Lord's brother," as well as others (Stephen, Philip, Barnabas, Mark, Silas, Timothy), its two greatest heroes are Peter and Paul. Peter's story is told through Chapter *12*, and he reappears at the council in Jerusalem in Chapter *15*.

Paul's story begins near the end of Chapter 7, at the stoning of Stephen, and *ends with him in Rome, proclaiming the kingdom of God*. And there it concludes. Although Acts was written after the martyrdom of both Peter and Paul, it ends on a note of triumph and doesn't speak of their deaths.

Note, then, not only the biographical aspects of Acts but also the *geographical* aspects (and have these in mind, incidentally, when we come to the book of Revelation). Acts 1:8 sets the trajectory: "You shall be my witnesses in Jerusalem and in all Judea and Samaria and to the end of the earth." *Rome*, where the book concludes, after recounting the apostles' work in Jerusalem, Judea, and Samaria, is in fact the jumping-off point for "the end of the earth." *What Acts recounts is how the center of the church's gravity shifted from Jerusalem to Rome.* As the author knew, Jerusalem's church had disappeared from that city during the Roman conquest in the year 71.

Acts, then, is about *Peter, Paul,* and *Rome*, with Paul triumphantly "preaching the kingdom of God and teaching about the Lord Jesus Christ quite openly and unhindered" *in Rome.*

4. *"The Catholic Epistles"*: *James, 1 and 2 Peter, 1, 2, and 3 John, Jude.* In his Epistle to the Galatians, Paul speaks (not in the most flattering terms) of the "pillars" of the church in Jerusalem, whom he lists in this order: "James, and Cephas [i.e., 'Peter'] and John" (2:9). It is no coincidence that, after Hebrews (and almost picking up where Hebrews left off in its opening address "to the twelve tribes in the Dispersion"), we have the Epistle of James, followed by the letters of Peter and John — *in that order*, which reflects the order of those same Jerusalem leaders in Galatians. And then, almost as an afterthought, we have the Epistle of Jude, "servant of Jesus Christ and brother of James" (1:1). Jude is placed here, an addendum to the three "pillars" in Jerusalem, because he is the brother of James and thus shares something of his

authority, although he is not one of the "pillars" whom Paul lists. With the Catholic Epistles, we have in a sense moved backward geographically, from Rome to Jerusalem the mother church, with its venerable apostolic "pillars," each of whom had known Jesus personally. As already noted, Paul's authority and his "scriptures" are guaranteed in the canon by no one less than Peter himself (2 Pet. 3:15–16; the question of the authorship of 2 Peter is not pertinent to this discussion).

5. The book of Revelation. The NT concludes with a single work of prophecy. Even though scholars make distinctions between "apocalyptic literature" and "prophetic literature," neither Jews nor Christians distinguished between these overlapping genres. Just as the OT in the Christian Bible has the Prophets positioned as the last section of the canon, so the NT has the book of the Revelation ("Apocalypse") to John as its conclusion. One among many early Christian and Jewish apocalypses, the canonical worthiness of Revelation was long disputed. Athanasius seems to have been the one who decided finally in its favor, including it in his canonical list in 367. One reason for its inclusion in the fourth century, after Constantine's (and Julian the Apostate's) reign, may have been because it was understood to have been partially fulfilled by the Empire's embrace of Christianity: "The kingdom of the world [the Roman 'world,' that is] has become the kingdom of our Lord and of his Christ, and he shall reign for ever and ever" (11:15). Revelation may be viewed as taking the NT trajectory to its ultimate destination. If Acts had taken the church *from Jerusalem to Rome* (and "to the end of the earth"), Revelation takes it *from Rome to the New Jerusalem.* With Revelation, the fourth-century canon not only looks back at the church's past, but also (as it understands it in light of the "Constantinian Privilege") at its present, and finally towards its future.

In conclusion, then, the result of the Christian development of the canon during the second and third centuries, with its rigorously applied criteria of antiquity, apostolicity, catholicity, and orthodoxy, is that our NT contains the oldest body of Christian literature in existence, carefully and reverently preserved. The fourth-century church gave it a canonical "shape," but the *contents* are the inheritance of the church's first-century faith.

APPENDIX 3
Lectio Divina

There is a *right* way to read the Bible in Christian tradition. It is sound, intelligent, "spiritual," and it dates to the earliest centuries. I will be unequivocal on the point: what I outline below is the authentic practice — developed, schematized, and refined over time, certainly, but essentially, it's the "way" of reading the sacred texts that would have been recognizable, until relatively recently, to Hebrews and Christians alike. For example, we find Paul (rabbi and apostle) employing a form of it in his letters whenever he "exegetes" passages from the Old Testament — and we should not fail to notice that he never once explains these texts as a modern interpreter would. For Paul, they are "spiritual" and, most often, allegorical. Now, I'm not saying that other ways of reading the Bible haven't become customary in a variety of contexts over the past five hundred years; I am saying, though, that those other ways are not the *right* way — not right, at any rate, if one wants to understand what Origen (c. 185–c. 253) meant when he likened the "eating" of scripture to partaking of the Eucharist, so that in turn (as Henri de Lubac explained) it might "unlock the divine secret hidden in our heart" (quoted in Špidlík 1986).[1] I dare say, the traditional Christian method of reading the Bible among modern-day Christians is something of a lost art, and the consequences of that failure have been grim.

In the case of biblical fundamentalism, the damage inflicted has been long-lasting and grievously harmful. Those who have reacted against it, sometimes

---

[1] Tomáš Špidlík, SJ, *The Spirituality of the Christian East: A Systematic Handbook*, trans. Anthony P. Gythiel (Kalamazoo, 1986), 5.

intemperately, have had just cause. In the Protestant world, the Bible has often been regarded as "the Word of God" without necessary qualification or caveat, read as a flat univocal text, and considered the *only* foundation for faith and practice. This ahistorical, untraditional, and *illiterate* way of reading the scriptures now appears to many — again, quite wrongly — to be the indisputable standard; both believers and unbelievers alike assume it to be so, which is why secular critics of the Bible usually come across like reverse-fundamentalists. Whenever one hears the unsurprisingly ignorant claim that the Bible — usually in reference to the Hebrew Bible or Old Testament, although the New Testament comes in for its fair share of lumps, too — is just a "Bronze Age" production with a particularly nasty deity at its center, the chief blame for that widespread impression falls squarely on the shoulders of biblical literalists.

My focus in what follows will be that mystical tradition of reading scripture which has deep patristic and monastic roots — monastic, because in the Middle Ages literacy was preserved and taught in the monasteries. At the heart of monastic ascetical practice was what came to be known in the Latin West as *lectio divina*, or "holy reading." It was also the practice in the Greek and Syriac East, which was its cradle, but not schematized with the same precision as it was to become in the Latin context.

Lectio divina was not confined to the reading of scripture. Other revered literature was also included in its purview. But primarily and most importantly, the books of the Old and New Testaments were "devoured" as spiritual food, and they nourished the "eater" with their life-giving nutrients for sustaining mystical life. *Lectio divina* was, without question, at the *very heart* of spiritual practice. For any reading these words who might have been battered by fundamentalism's abusive use of the Bible in the past, this may seem inconceivable. But earlier Christians, whatever other deficiencies they may have had in their particular times and places, weren't literalists, and the ugly, debased fundamentalism we find so prevalent in our own society happily was unknown to them. The Bible was integral to spiritual tradition *and could only be appreciated rightly within the context of liturgical and mystical prayer*. Indeed, there were some portions of the Bible that were deemed unedifying, even for monks, and were considered too morally problematic to be for general consumption (as I said, these were not fundamentalists; they had a keen sense of moral propriety). This sensitivity in discriminating between what was useful and beneficial in the scriptures and what was not dates to the earliest centuries of Christianity. The Bible was not considered to be a "flat" or univocal book, and not everything in that vast collection of texts was thought to be profitable spiritually.

This basic, rather obvious, and thoroughly honest insight might be the first thing we could recover to our benefit. The Bible is not simply a "good book"; it's a complicated library of books, not without ambiguity, and it can't be reduced to any single neat system of ideas. That may frustrate those who believe in that exotic mythical beast called "biblical theology" (as if anything so consistent or concrete could emerge from that literary convergence of differing perspectives and genres, all of them in flux and affected by numerous outside cultural influences over the course of ages), but—perhaps paradoxically—it's also why so much of it is conducive to engendering profound insight when read rightly.

So, then, how do we read it *rightly*?

To begin with, we will consider the "senses" of scripture, of which there are *two*, the second comprised of *three* "sub-senses." As I've already noted, the idea that there can be layered "senses" in the texts we read was commonplace in antiquity. Some written texts, of course, have no depth, no "layers" of meaning. Take a grocery list for an example. It is what it is, the instructions for assembling your latest IKEA purchase are as literal as any text can possibly be, and so on. Other texts, however, whether poetry or prose or drama (the ancients loved plays), could be and, in fact, most often *should* be read on multiple levels. The two most obvious levels are the *literal* level and the *metaphorical* or *representational* level. Ancient readers of Homer, for example, read the *Iliad* and the *Odyssey* both as "ripping yarns" of mythological history and as spiritually enlightening texts. This two-level reading of many texts has always been part of literature (and drama, cinema, and television, as well). We take it for granted, whether we are conscious of it or not. The problem with literalism, of course, is that it doesn't go further than the first level. That would be fine if the text is a grocery list, say, or a tourist guide, or the IKEA instruction booklet I mentioned. But spiritual texts, or texts that are at least read for spiritual purposes, like serious literature of all kinds, cannot be read simply on that level. The literal level is the primary one, of course, but there are deeper levels to be plumbed.

It's important to understand what *literal* meant in the ancient world and, in fact, still means today. There's some confusion about its meaning among fundamentalists, who assume that a poetic (and rather late) text such as the first chapter of Genesis, which uses parallelism masterfully to describe the essentially indescribable appearance of all things, is *literally* true. That the text has *meaning* has never been in dispute; but it's never been understood, even by its ancient readers, as a simple description of "what really happened." Any claim that the Bible contains science as we know it or the sort of historiography that we are used to, which is only a few centuries old, is an *illiterate* claim. However, the *literal* sense is basic to reading, even to "spiritual reading." What *literal* means is simply this: *what the text actually says on the surface level.* It has nothing to do with whether the thing, event, or person described in a given text is fact or fiction. The literal reading of this passage from *Tarzan of the Apes* by Edgar Rice Burroughs is plain enough: "As the body rolled to the ground Tarzan of the Apes placed his foot upon the neck of his lifelong enemy and, raising his eyes to the full moon, threw back his fierce young head and voiced the wild and terrible cry of his people." That's very, very literal. It's also utterly fictional (and not at all metaphorical). Reading that sentence literally, we don't need to believe in its veracity.

The clearest statement about reading the scriptures according to the two senses (and three sub-senses) is found in the fourteenth conference of John Cassian's *Conferences*. Cassian (c. 360–c. 435) and his companion, Germanus, are being instructed by the desert monk, Abba Nesteros, "a man of the highest knowledge and outstanding in every regard."[2] He is teaching them about "contemplating the secrets of invisible mysteries," and he says that, in order for that to happen, they must learn to practice "a defined order and method." He makes a twofold distinction, between *theoretike* ("which consists in the contemplation of divine things and in the understanding of most sacred meanings") and *praktike* (i.e., what can be "practiced," "practical": "which reaches its fulfillment in correction of behavior and in cleansing from vice"): "Whoever, therefore, wishes to attain to the *theoretike* must first pursue practical knowledge with all his strength and power. For the *praktike* can be possessed without the theoretical [i.e., contemplation], but the theoretical can never be seized without the practical." In other words, the *moral* life is integral to the full experience of *contemplation*. It is in relation to this subject of the practical and the theoretical (or contemplative) that Abba Nesteros teaches them about the *senses* of spiritual reading—and, in fact, uses Paul's treatment of the Old Testament (in Galatians 4 and 1 Corinthians 10, specifically) as a model.

---

[2] John Cassian, *The Conferences*, trans. and annotated by Boniface Ramsey, O. P. (Mahwah, 1997), 505.

The *literal* sense, then, is the place for exegesis: what we can unpack "out of" the text — what it is telling us on the surface. Whether it's history, legend, parable, poetry, prophecy, etc., we are only concerned with the details (including words, context, cultural and historical background, and so on) of the text. At this stage, help from commentaries, the notes in a (good) study Bible, lexicons, and so on may come in handy. But a word of caution: *lectio divina* should not become a formal study. Study is fine in its place, even to be encouraged, but *lectio* proper must stay mentally contemplative and therefore more concerned with the spiritual senses.

Besides the *literal* reading, there are "three kinds of spiritual knowledge" — the "sub-senses" I mentioned. In other words, what I have been calling the "metaphorical" level of reading, Abba Nesteros calls the *spiritual* level, and he breaks this category into three sorts: the allegorical, the tropological (or moral), and the anagogical.[3]

The *allegorical* is the level at which "the things that the historical [literal] narrative conceals are laid bare by a spiritual understanding and explanation."[4] The *allegorical* sense takes us from the level of "what's explicitly on the page" to what the text signifies. For example, the Song of Solomon is literally a collection of erotic poems that may or may not have originally been written with allegorical intent; either way, it can be read simply as love poetry. The rabbis included it in the Hebrew canon because they saw in it an allegory of God's love for the people of Israel. Origen and other early Christian exegetes transferred this essentially Judaic perspective to Christ and his "bride," the church; and — more personally still — they applied the analogy to Christ and the individual soul (a "mystical" interpretation that continued throughout the patristic, medieval, and later ages). Images of battle in the Psalms and elsewhere were routinely interpreted as the interior

---

[3] Ibid., 509.
[4] Ibid., 510.

struggle with our passions, thoughts, and the powers of evil (and some of us continue unapologetically to pray the rougher Psalms in precisely this way). The parables of Jesus — though some quibble about the term — are allegorical (and many of the Gospel stories *about* Jesus certainly have allegorical connotations). Paul's treatment of the Hebrew Bible, as we noted, is almost exclusively allegorical.

The *tropological* or moral level is that at which "we discern by a prudent examination everything that pertains to practical discretion, in order to see whether it is useful and good."[5] This sense is where we ponder how we are to live our lives, in the light of what we read. Jesus incisively addressed the state of our "heart" — that "from within" ourselves come the motivations of evil actions. Jesus, incidentally, was no easy comforter in that regard; he accepted his followers "as they were," but with the proviso that their lives would henceforth mean the continuous transformation of their hearts inwardly and behavior outwardly. The idea of an all-inclusive Jesus — meaning "everything is permitted" by him — has no basis in the Gospels. He certainly invites us to follow him, but the stipulation is that we do what we are obliged to do if we intend to be made whole. One shouldn't read the Gospels and overlook that central aspect.

The *anagogical* level is that at which the words of scripture "are directed to the invisible and to what lies in the future" — that is to say, to our "end" or *ultimate aim* (what Abba Moses, in Cassian's very first conference, called our *telos*, contrasting it with our *immediate aim — skopos —* which is to become self-disciplined). The *anagogical* has to do with the hope that accompanies the other two spiritual senses — that we are in a process, "mirroring the Lord's glory... being transformed into the same image, from glory to glory, as by the Lord, the Spirit" (2 Cor. 3:18, DBHNT). We are put in mind of "resurrection," "eternal

---

[5] Ibid., 511.

life," "the age to come," "the fullness of time," "when that which is perfect has come," "when God is all in all," and, of course, "the judgment"—remembering that all these phrases and images are metaphors for what is inconceivable to us on this side of things. *Lectio divina* finds its fullest significance where the anagogical is concerned.

So, at the heart of devotional practice we have this layered reading of sacred texts; ruminating on them, chewing them, devouring them, we assimilate their transformative nutrients. Again, not every text of scripture is conducive to this process, nor does every text carry all four levels of meaning. Some texts of the Bible, as Origen and others were forthright in acknowledging, are morally problematic and can't easily be used for spiritual nourishment.

No spiritual "method" works mechanically. That should be said before moving on to a more detailed discussion of the method of *lectio divina*. Christian "sacred reading," as defined within the Tradition, is when God is perceived as present and communing with the "heart" (or mind) through the text. It requires of us a prepared state of inner receptivity. Another name for this inner state is "recollection" or, more aptly, *re-collection*. One *re-collects* one's scattered thoughts and, in interior silence, gives undivided attention to the sacred page. In heightened experiences of this practice, the Spirit (or "Breath") of God is felt to be—as "in the beginning" of all things—creatively brooding over the chaotic deep within the depths of the reader. (The New Testament uses graphic language about our inner depths, by the way: σπλάγχνα—"*splagchna*" and κοιλία—"*koilia*" refer to the guts or intestines in the first instance, and to the belly and the womb in the second; all that we mean by the "unconscious," including the dark, untamed, disturbingly irrational aspects of our hidden selves, can be associated with such imagery without too much conceptual strain.)

The sole purpose of this sort of attentive, spiritually alert concentration is, as we've said, communion with God. It isn't "Bible study"; it isn't done—if one is ordained—for the sake of preparing a homily; it isn't done to gain an objectively "correct" understanding of a given text. It isn't, in other words, an intellectual undertaking or for the accrual of "Bible knowledge." It is *subjective* in the purest sense; one is preparing to be acted upon, not to act. One prepares oneself simply to *receive* and to *listen*. And "to listen" in the biblical/patristic/monastic vocabulary has as its aim a *co-operation*—"synergy"—with the action of the Spirit ("work out your own salvation in reverence and trembling, for it is God who is making active within you both the willing and the working of that which is dearly desirable"; Philippians 2:12c–13, DBHNT). That's the state of mind necessary for practicing *lectio divina*.

The effectiveness of the method, then, depends a great deal on our inner preparedness before we engage in it each day. There should be nothing hasty about the practice; we should give it all the time it takes. For it truly to assist in our "transformation by the renewal of our intellect" (see Rom. 12:3), it ought to become part of our regular routine—our personal "rule (*regula*) of life." We will realize its mounting influence in our lives over time. In the words of Peter of Damascus (twelfth century), "We who do no more than listen to the Scriptures, should devote ourselves to them and meditate on them so constantly that through our persistence a longing for God is impressed upon our hearts, as St Maximos [the Confessor] says."[6] As with any serious discipline, then, its value can only be ascertained over the long haul.

When it comes to the actual practice of *lectio divina*, one of the clearest texts on the subject is the work of the great Carthusian, Guigo II "the Angelic" (d. 1188), the ninth prior of Grand Chartreuse.[7] His short text,

---

[6] Nikodemos of the Holy Mountain and Makarios of Corinth, comp., *The Philokalia: The Complete Text*, trans. from the Greek and ed. G. E. H. Palmer, Philip Sherrard, and Kallistos Ware, vol. 3, 123.
[7] He is called "Guigo II" to distinguish him from Guigo I, the fifth prior, and Guigo de Ponte, who lived a century later. Those

The Ladder of Monks, addressed to a brother named Gervase, lists four steps in the practice of *lectio divina*: *lectio* (reading), *meditatio* (meditation—which will need some clarification), *oratio* (prayer), and *contemplatio* (contemplation).[8] It's an engaging text, written with warmth and charm—not uncommon during this golden period of healthy, flourishing, and humane Western monasticism. He introduces the subject in this inviting way:

> One day when I was busy working with my hands I began to think about our spiritual work, and all at once four stages in spiritual exercise came into my mind: reading, meditation, prayer and contemplation. These make a ladder for monks by which they are lifted up from earth to heaven. It has few rungs, yet its length is immense and wonderful, for its lower end rests upon the earth, but its top pierces the clouds and touches heavenly secrets...
>
> Reading is the careful study of the Scriptures, concentrating all one's powers on it. Meditation is the busy application of the mind to seek with the help of one's own reason for knowledge of hidden truth. Prayer is the heart's devoted turning to God to drive away evil and obtain what is good. Contemplation is when the mind is in some sort lifted up to God and held above itself, so that it tastes the joys of everlasting sweetness.[9]

"Meditation" in this instance refers to a process of rational thought. It means "to ponder" or "consider." Guigo compares it in his letter to chewing: *masticatio* or

---

who have seen the film *Into Great Silence*—German title, *Die große Stille*—will, no doubt, recall the majestic monastery of Grand Chartreuse and its surroundings.

[8] Another medieval writer, Hugo of St Victor, an older contemporary of Guigo and an Augustinian canon, added a fifth step between *oratio* and *contemplatio*: *operatio*, or the doing of good works. Quite rightly, he saw that contemplative practice cannot be divorced from charitable action and "the works of mercy."

[9] Guigo II, *The Ladder of Monks: A Letter on the Contemplative Life and Twelve Meditations*, trans. and intro. Edmund Colledge, O.S.A. and James Walsh, S.J. (London: Oxford, 1978), 81–82.

"mastication" (an analogy dating back to Origen and even further back to the scriptures: see Eze. 3:1; Rev. 10:10). William of St Thierry (first a Benedictine and later a Cistercian), another earlier contemporary of Guigo, referred to it as *ruminatio* — like a cow chomping on her cud, swallowing it, and bringing it back up for more chewing: "Some part of your daily reading should also each day be committed to memory, taken in as it were into the stomach, to be more carefully digested and brought up again for frequent rumination; something... helpful to concentration, something that will take hold of the mind and save it from distraction."[10] Since reading was usually performed out loud in ancient and medieval times, and muttered to oneself when in private (not a bad practice to have even today), the thought of the "mouth" chewing on a text came quite naturally to these writers. Guigo, then, continues with the analogy of "eating" the text as he describes the four steps of *lectio*:

> Reading, as it were, puts food whole into the mouth, meditation chews it and breaks it up, prayer extracts its flavor, contemplation is the sweetness itself which gladdens and refreshes. Reading works on the outside, meditation on the pith; prayer asks for what we long for, contemplation gives us delight in the sweetness which we have found.[11]

He then provides an example of how these four aspects apply to a particular scripture. He takes the single line, "Blessed are the pure in heart, for they shall see God" (Matt. 5:8), and then walks us through the process. "This is a short text of Scripture," he explains, "but it is of great sweetness, like a grape that is put into the mouth filled with many senses to feed the soul." During the practice, Guigo pictures the reader pausing, "wishing to have a

---

[10] Theodore Berkeley, OCSO, trans., *The Golden Epistle: A Letter to the Brethren of Mont Dieu*, vol. 4, *The Works of William of St Thierry*, intro. J. M. Déchanet, OSB (Kalamazoo, 1980), 52.

[11] Guigo, *Ladder of Monks*, 82–83.

fuller understanding of this [text]," and beginning "to bite and chew upon this grape, as though putting it in a wine press, while it [the mind] stirs up its powers of reasoning..." This becomes, then, the act of meditation, no longer remaining "on the outside." One's mind is "not detained by unimportant things, climbs higher, goes to the heart of the matter, examines each point carefully." He describes the many insights one might gain through meditation but then adds a word of caution. One is not to stop here; this isn't the end of the process.

> Do you see how much juice has come from one little grape, how great a fire has been kindled from a spark, how this small piece of metal, "Blessed are the pure in heart, for they shall see God," has acquired a new dimension by being hammered out on the anvil of meditation? And even more might be drawn from it at the hands of someone truly expert. I feel that "the well is deep," but I am still an ignorant beginner, and it is only with difficulty that I have found something in which to draw up these few drops.... [F]rom this [the soul] deduces how sweet it would be to know by experience the purity that meditation has shown to be so full of joy.
>
> But what is it to do? It is consumed with longing, yet it can find no means of its own to have what it longs for; and the more it searches the more it thirsts. *As long as it is meditating, so long is it suffering, because it does not feel that sweetness which, as meditation shows, belongs to purity of heart, but which it does not give.*[12]

In other words, the rational process will leave one high and dry—unfulfilled and still empty—unless it motivates the reader to go on to the other two stages. "So the soul," Guigo writes, "seeing that it cannot attain by itself to that sweetness of knowing and feeling for which it longs...humbles itself and betakes itself to prayer..."[13] Through prayer (the third stage), the reader stills himself,

---

[12] Ibid., 85. Emphasis added.
[13] Ibid., 86.

assumes a posture of attentiveness and concentration, perhaps using a repeated word or phrase to subdue and restrain straying thoughts, and in that silent act of longing and expectation, awaits the grace of contemplation. "[God] slakes [the soul's] thirst, He feeds its hunger, He makes the soul forget all earthly things: by making it die to itself He gives it new life in a wonderful way, *and by making it drunk He brings it back to its true senses.*"[14] In the contemplative state, Guigo tells the reader he may experience the gift of tears: "an outward washing proceeds from the inner cleansing...our inward stains are cleansed, by which the fires of our sins are put out."[15] Other interior stirrings may occur as the divine presence makes itself evident, to which he can put no descriptive words:

> Why do we try to express in everyday language affections that no language can describe? *Those who have not known such things do not understand them*, for they could learn more clearly of them *only from the book of experience* where God's grace itself is the teacher. Otherwise it is of no use for the reader to search in earthly books: there is little sweetness in the study of the literal sense, unless there be a commentary, *which is found in the heart, to reveal the inward sense.*[16]

This last statement is a bold one and true. To understand something of what goes on within an individual engaged in the act of contemplation, one must practice contemplation oneself. "Only the book of experience" will do. Guigo is clear that the literal sense all by itself of scripture has limited if any real value (and, as we know, it can also do positive harm). *Lectio divina* is *deep reading.* It takes time, and it requires effort, meditative "mastication," prayer, moral and mental discipline, and silent contemplation. Its benefits to the soul, however, are beyond measure.

---

[14] Ibid., 87. Emphasis added.
[15] Ibid., 88.
[16] Ibid., 89. Emphasis added.

ADDISON HODGES HART is the author of eleven books, nine non-fictional (theology, biblical exegesis, art history, and biography) and two fictional (a novel and a collection of short stories). His two most recent works, published by Angelico Press, are *The Voyage of Life: The Sacred Vision of Thomas Cole* and *Patapsco Spirits: Eleven Ghost Stories* (both published in 2023). A retired priest and university chaplain, he was received into the Orthodox Church in 2024. He currently resides in Norway. (He also has a lively, easy-to-access Substack page, *The Pragmatic Mystic*.)